# Trans Forming Families:

## Real Stories About Transgendered Loved Ones

### Second Edition
*Updated and Expanded*

## Mary Boenke
### Editor

**Foreword by Ari Ishtar Lev**
**Introduction by Jessica Xavier**

I see a beautiful butterfly emerging. The caterpillar was nice and I miss him, but the butterfly is so gentle, so peaceful, so softly radiant, that I almost don't remember the warm, fuzzy, little guy. The butterfly will be so wonderful once her wings are fully spread into the sun...

Jackie Greer, *Trans Forming Families*

# TRANS FORMING FAMILIES:
Real Stories About Transgendered Loved Ones
2nd Edition, updated and expanded

Mary Boenke, Editor

Oak Knoll Press
180 Bailey Blvd.
Hardy, VA 24101

Copy Editor -- Daphne Reed
Cover Art   -- Delores Dudley
                Lori Bowden
Consultant -- Yvonne Y. Miller

Printed in the United States of America,
February 2003

Library of Congress Card Catalogue Number: 98-89891
ISBN:  0-615-12307-4

# This book is lovingly dedicated

to our own brave son

who has dared to be true to himself

and taught us so much,

To all those brave, pioneering

transgendered persons who have risked

family, employment and life itself

for their own internal integrity,

To all those courageous families,

open to ambiguity and new frontiers,

who hold  love more important

than social and religious custom,

and

To my own husband and family,

whose love and patience

are exemplary.

# CONTENTS
### * Denotes pseudonym

## VI. TRANSGENDERED PEOPLE AS PARENTS

## PART VII. THERAPISTS' COMMENTS

# PREFACE and ACKNOWLEDGMENTS

This collection originally took shape in 1996 when I first began realizing the high rate of families who reject their transgendered loved ones. While I was involved in organizing the Transgender Network for PFLAG (Parents, Families and Friends of Lesbians and Gays) a number of families who proudly accepted their trans members came forward. It seemed important to make these positive stories available to all those who were struggling with much misinformation, often with pain and anger as well. The first edition has sold out and many kind readers have persuaded me to produce this second edition.

Some of the stories in the first four sections of the first volume have been replaced. Three new sections have been added-- brief autobiographies by trans persons themselves, experiences of trans persons as parents, and a few articles by therapists who work with transgenders. While the book as a whole, I believe, represents balance and diversity, this was not possible within each section. It is, also, truly impossible to represent every type of situation and experience; we are all so different and unique. As before, FTM and MTF transsexuals, crossdressers and intersexed people are included; some who chose to live closer to the middle ground have been added. I hope each reader will find some stories here that are similar enough to his or her situation to be useful.

My husband and I feel fortunate to have three wonderful, healthy adult children, with two just-right spouses and five bouncy grandchildren. We also feel grateful to our middle "child" who came out to us after freshman year of college as a lesbian and again in her late 30s as a transman. Both revelations came as complete surprises, and while it took us a while to "get with it" the first time, there never was any question about loving and accepting her. By the time of the second outing we were active with PFLAG, knew very well the process parents and families often go through--shock, anger, guilt, grief, bargaining, acceptance, and more--and were able to travel the often painful road to understanding very quickly. Being a Unitarian-Universalist and a social worker certainly gave me a headstart in the acceptance process.

In PFLAG we often say there is one more stage-- celebration! It really is true! We are impressed with our new son who seemed to handle his gender transition very gracefully, in spite of the fact it must seem like jumping off the end of the world. We are also grateful to him for introducing to us, twice now, new worlds and wonderful people we had never before dreamed of. We would not change our son in any way, even if we could, nor would we have missed these journeys for anything in the world! (For our personal stories, please see my husband's chapter, "Letter to Allen," page 41, and my own very positive PFLAG experiences, page 30.)

So compelling is the need for inner and outer congruity that many transgenders who make these changes risk enormous personal losses -- career, spouses, children, and/or family of origin. We hope this book will make some small contribution toward reducing at least the risk of losing one's family.

Of course, there would be no book without the brave and loving authors themselves, whom I regard both as trans-pioneers and valued friends. We have not sought out the best known transgenders, who are already well published, but rather those "ordinary-extraordinary" folks, with whom we hope readers new to transgender issues can identify. The well-established authors on the back cover have been most supportive.

I want, especially, to thank several others-- Jessica Xavier for generously compiling and updating the Glossary, Trans Organizations and Bibliography, as well as writing a fine Introduction. Ari Ishtar Lev has written a very kind and informative Foreword, Daphne Reed has been my indespensible, sharp-eyed proof reader, and Yvonne Miller, a savvy supporter. I am solely responsible for any remaining flaws, including choice of materials, editing, lay-out, and probably much more.

I am happy to forward mail to authors or poets in this book or on the back cover and to receive reader's comments. (See last page.)

Mary Boenke
Hardy, VA
December 2002

# FOREWORD

I picked up the first edition of Mary Boenke's Trans Forming Families at the True Spirit Conference three years ago, and while we drove home on that snowy February afternoon, I read the book aloud to my partner. Laughing in sections, tearful in others, I knew that I held a treasure in my hand. I bought a few copies and began handing them out to friends and clients. I wanted everyone to read this book—I wanted it on the required reading list of every high school in America!

Let's face it: transgenderism and transsexualism are confusing to most people and make them feel profoundly uncomfortable. Limited to the information available on sensational television shows, trans people are seen as weird, mentally ill, kinky, and perhaps even dangerous. In desperate need of a better press agent, the transgender community found a powerful ally in Mary Boenke. Her heartwarming collection of stories by the family members of transgendered, transsexual, androgyne, and intersexed people serves to put a personal face on transgenderism.

What could be more healing --like warm soup on a cold day--than the words of the people who know transgendered people best, who love them the most, than their own families! The stories in this book are written by men and women, mothers and fathers, siblings and spouses, grandparents and children of trans-identified people. Mary Boenke is herself the mother of a transgendered son, as well as a retired social worker, and a member of PFLAG. She understands all too well the inner journey of discovery that family members of transgendered people experience. It is not just the transgendered person who moves through a coming out process, what I call an "emergence" process, but those who love them are also powerfully impacted by transition.

Writing a book is hard work; I know this because I have just completed two books, one on counseling with transgendered people (Transgender Emergence, Haworth Press) and the other on parenting in the LGBT community (How Queer, Penguin Press). Mary Boenke has done an extraordinary job collecting the stories of men and women, mothers and fathers, siblings and spouses, grandparents and children of trans-identified people.

I am privileged to work as a family therapist with families of transgendered people. I have sat with a 60-year old man, a farmer wearing worn work boots, who kept wringing his gnarled hands while he told me how confused he was about his ten-year old granddaughter who wore boy's clothes and insisted that she wanted to be man when she grew up. He sat on the edge of my couch, uncomfortable to be in a professional office talking to a stranger, but he had driven two hours to the big city to see me, someone who might be able to help him understand. He loved his granddaughter deeply and wanted to know if she was "like this" because of her parents' divorce. With his voice cracking he wanted to know what would happen to this child; he prayed she would "only" be gay.

I have worked with crossdressing men whose wives think they are having an affair with another woman because they found lipstick and women's underwear in the car. I have worked with young trans kids who are buying hormones on the Internet but refuse to tell their parents. I work with many, many middle-aged men who took the risk and told their spouses that they had been living with a secret for two decades of their marriage. Some of these marriages have survived disclosure, moving to greater depth, honestly, and understanding. Others have ended, with irate spouses filing for, and winning, sole custody of children. I work with women who used to be male professionals making $500,000 a year, and are now praying they will get a job as a telemarketer at $8 an hour. I work with gallant FtM's, who have somehow managed to incorporate the best of lesbian-feminist politics into their masculine identities, and whose lesbian lovers have moved from anger, to sadness, to acceptance, and eventually into passion.

Sadly, I have also buried clients, one a victim of a violent crime, whose family said, "I knew it would come to this," and the other, who had much familial support, but simply couldn't handle another day of fighting for her dignity. Families move through predictable stages when they realize or discover that a family member is gender-variant. They experience turmoil and emotional upheaval, and then begin a process of negotiation to learn more about trans issues. Finally, if they are willing to take the journey, they come to a place of acceptance, compassion, and transformation; they find balance, integrating their loved one back into their hearts and families.

The book you are holding, *Trans Forming Families: Real Stories About Transgendered Loved Ones*, is written by family members who have moved through this emotional process and have come to a place of understanding. Filled with loving accounts of parents trying to support their trans children, couples re-inventing their relationships within a new gender paradigm, and therapists committed to serving as compassionate advocates, we finally have more personal and intimate portrayals of trans people's transition process, and the truth about trans lives. The truth is that trans people's lives are embedded within families, many of whom are loving and supportive.

Expanded and more inclusive than the first edition, this is an extraordinary collection of stories, a kind of herbal medicine for trans families. Mary Boenke's anthology shows us that families can not only survive transition, but more importantly, they are transformed, themselves, in the process.

Arlene (Ari) Istar Lev
Family therapist, educator, activist
Albany, NY
December 2002

# INTRODUCTION

It has been a little more than four years since the first edition of *Trans Forming Families* was published, and in that time so much has happened. More and more transgendered persons have come out, bringing more and more of their parents, spouses, partners, children and other family members with them. We are in the midst of an explosion of increased interest and public information about transgendered people. More cities have been adding gender identity and expression to their antidiscrimination ordinances. Along with increased recognition in public polls, it seems we are making real progress in the all-important battle for hearts and minds.

Our gender education presentations have grown in scale and sophistication. We can now place transgendered experience into a broad, behavioral context that secures our connection with the rest of humanity. We can show others how different forms of gender variance are manifested across a wide range of social identities and sexual orientations. Many more ways to be gender variant have emerged, and thus there are many more gender variant people than we trans folks once believed! And our presentations and educational materials are becoming more customized to the specific needs of various audiences that listen to us and read them. However, in so many of our presentations, we still are asked that same question, "What about your family?"

Although familial acceptance seems to be slowly in-creasing, rejection is still a common experience for many trans people, especially older ones. The loss of half of my birth family in gender transition was extremely painful for me, as well as for them. But that pain led me to PFLAG's Transgender Network (TNet) where I found parents and grandparents, brothers and sisters, friends, spouses and partners of transsexual and trans-gendered men and women. I found a group of people working out the many issues that families suddenly face when their son or daughter, brother or sister, spouse or partner, parent or grand-child tells them the words that few family member ever want or expect to hear. In our large and still growing TNet family, we are finding some answers for the rush of questions that follow in the wake of a disclosure that one of our own is transgendered.

Despite our progress, gender education is still a challenging endeavor. For almost all people, gender follows one's birth sex, and thus it's a given, to be quickly taken for granted. This one obvious fact is the foundation for the wall of ignorance that surrounds not only transgendered people, but also gender itself. Although gender governs the full spectrum of human behaviors, almost all people are wholly unconscious of it. Thus gender is also an unspoken and unwritten social contract that all people enter into without much discussion or debate. Gender is simply the way things are--for men and women, and for boys and girls.

For transgendered people it's not that simple. We can spend half our lifetimes struggling to understand who we truly are, and the other half becoming who we were meant to be. Ours is usually an internal war, which we keep hidden from others because of our shame, guilt, and isolation. In simple terms, it's a struggle for our real selves--finally to become complete human beings. Contrary to conventional wisdom, we transgendered are not confused--we know who we are. But we are confusing to a culture that labels the transcendence of sex and gender as a mental disorder and our gender variance as a psychopathology. If we are fortunate, in time we come to see our gender differences not as burdens but as special gifts. If we are a little more fortunate, in time the rest of humankind will come to value us for those gifts, for we can help them heal from their own gender wars.

With this second edition, Mary Boenke and her contributors have found even more new answers to that inevitable question, "What about your family?" While every family is different, many represented herein have struggled to come to terms of acceptance of their transgendered loved ones, who may be children, adolescents or fully grown adults. But there is so much more than mere struggle here, beyond the shame, guilt and confusion, and the simple difficulties of getting used to new names and pronouns. Parents grieving the loss of their child, mixed with the joyous discovery of another child they never knew. Whole families learning new lessons while journeying with their transgendered voyagers through their new lives. Spouses and partners creating new understandings of committed relationships beyond the obsolete definitions and irrelevant legalities in their stories of what it means to love a changeling. Children and siblings coming to see their trans parents and trans siblings as unexpected blessings in their lives. Throughout these pages there is indeed much to celebrate, as these butterflies emerge transformed from their chrysalis and spread newly gendered wings over the world, held aloft by the love and courage of their families and their loved ones. And it is that special, transformative love that marks PFLAGers everywhere.

Yet many other families still live in the shadows of misunderstanding, estranged from their transgendered loved ones. I pray this book will find its way into their hands and open their hearts, as they discover themselves in its pages, in the personal stories of these courageous contributors. When I get discouraged about the pace of social change and societal acceptance, Mary likes to remind me that things really are getting better for transgendered people. She's right for many reasons, but especially because a mother's love knows no bounds, and her hopes for her children really do transcend all the misunderstanding and hatred of others. While we still have so much more work to do, and so much farther to go down this road so rarely traveled, I've no doubts this book will move us toward a future without fear that much faster.

Jessica Xavier
November 4, 2002
Kensington, Maryland

# PART I

# RAISING GENDER-VARIANT

# CHILDREN

# NAE
## Elisa Lurkis

*I am a grant writer who lives with my husband and two children in San Diego, California. I am spending this year in Albuquerque.*

I was sure that my first child would be a girl. Although I chose not to have my conviction scientifically confirmed through ultrasound, I was nonetheless so convinced that I told my friends and family to buy only "girl" clothes as baby gifts. So nobody was more surprised than I was to hear the words, "It's a boy!"

When my best friend called me in the hospital and asked, "So what's your daughter's name?" I giggled and replied, "Her name is Nathan." Little did I know how telling that response would become. But I soon got used to the idea that I had a son, and in fact, felt a strange sense of pride that my first born child was a boy.

For the first year and a half, Nathan's behavior, like most very young children, was relatively gender free. When he occasionally displayed a preference for toys, he tended to favor construction vehicles, and became adept at naming them, "That's a tractor, that's a bulldozer, that's a backhoe." And when he showed a preference for pretty women in his choice of baby-sitters, my husband and I would pat each other on our backs, because, at only eighteen months, our son was already behaving like a stud.

But then, seemingly out of the blue, when our son was two, he informed us that he was no longer Nathan, that we must address him as Madeline and that he would answer to nothing else. Still, we didn't think much of it. After all, children had large imaginations and we did not want to impart close-minded rigid messages about gender onto our two-year-old son. So much did we want to encourage our son to be himself that when he began displaying a fervid interest in make-up, I went to the drugstore and purchased him a child's make-up kit.

"He's artistic," I would tell people, slightly defensively, when they indicated through their facial expressions that they

3

didn't approve. "He's very tactile, he likes the color. It's not really about gender at all." Occasionally, a flicker of doubt would gnaw at me as I explained my son's interests for the umpteenth time to friends and family. But I brushed it away and chided myself for being a product of my own uptight generation. Nonetheless, Nathan/ Madeline's focus on all things feminine began to wear on me. We couldn't make a trip to the grocery store without his endless commentary on the women he saw.

"She's wearing lipstick and she's wearing lipstick," he would say, pointing a still chubby finger at the various women in the checkout line. "Don't point," I'd tell him, pushing his arm down, "It isn't nice." And then when we would return home, he would run straight to his room, shouting happily, "I'm gonna play with my make-up!"

After days turned into weeks and months of make-up play, I grew both concerned and bored with my son's focus. "Let's play with something else," I would suggest, "Why don't we go outside and I'll push you on the swing?" "Okay!" my ever enthused child said, and outside we would go. But once he was seated on the swing, while I pushed him back and forth, his focus would return.

"Tell me stories about make-up," he would demand. Needless to say, aside from the fact that the subject of make-up did not easily lend itself to the structure of narrative plot, I was not eager to indulge him anymore. I began to regret my earlier indulgences. Maybe I shouldn't have bought him his own make-up. Maybe I shouldn't have encouraged him to explore his own interests. Maybe, and I still cringed at the thought, I should have nipped this thing in the bud from the start. Maybe then it wouldn't have gotten so out of hand and my sweet little boy would be just a what? A little boy who stuffed whole chunks of his psyche down deep so that his repressed feeling would emerge later, totally inappropriately? A little boy who felt shame about his softer, less macho side? Because if there was one thing I felt absolutely certain of, (well, at least ninety-percent), it was that I did not create Nathan's -- um, well -- interests.

Nonetheless, we decided to try to curb Nathan's tendencies. Under the advice of a child psychiatrist, we began to tell Nathan that we liked him better in his boy clothes. We also began limiting his dress-up play to 30 minutes a day, in the hopes that his interests might quietly fade out.

They didn't. Our imposed limitations only served to make our child unhappy and weepy. Still we persisted, thinking that we were doing the right thing by preparing our child for a world which would accept him better if he fit in.

As two turned to three, and then four and five, Nathan's focus remained constant, in spite of our constraints. Buying shoes would always become highly emotional, since he always wanted the sparkly pretty shoes and not the spiderman or power ranger sneakers. He accepted our half hour limit on his dress-up play, but his school friends were primarily girls, and we were constantly saying no to his wishes for a Barbie lunch box or a Power-puff Girl backpack.

Until, finally, one night, I stopped fighting. I was painting my nails one night, and Nathan asked if I would paint his. I had done this before, under the pretense that it was another sign of his artistic nature. I began painting his nails "Gum Drop Pink" because he preferred that to the muted maroon that I had chosen for myself. And all of a sudden, I realized that my child was not simply artistic, although he certainly was that as well. Suddenly, years of repressed inklings turned into a full-blown realization that my child's feminine focus was not going to go away. Blinking back tears as I continued to paint my child's toenails, it hit me full force that while I had thought that I had a son, I really had a daughter.

I frantically telephoned my therapist and she generously squeezed me in for an emergency session. Once on the couch, I spent all 55 minutes crying for the son I had never had. But upon leaving her office, I realized that I was ready to face the next day as the mother of a transgendered child, prepared to face whatever challenges might come my way. Acceptance suddenly became much easier than resistance.

From that point on, my husband and I decided to let our child be who he needed to be, without any restrictions. And what emerged was a child who was no longer weepy and difficult, but who in fact became happy and even exuberant about life. Dressed in all things pink, our little "Nae", as we began calling her, became a socially confident and independent GIRL!!! And now our child is almost six, and while she still goes to school dressed as a boy (her choice), most days she comes home and immediately changes into pink flowered leggings and a Powerpuff girl's shirt. Her decision to go to school "as a boy" is based on her own sense that kids would laugh at her if she did otherwise.

Of course, we worry about what the future holds. We know that the older our child gets, the less receptive the world is going to be about her differences. But for now we are just taking it one day at a time. And we are bolstered by the conviction that our support and our love will be what our child needs to feel secure and confident, no matter who she turns out to be.

Lemon Drops
Emery C. Walters

Sunshine, lemon drops
Chocolate flavored tootsie pops
Ferries, cars, skates and bikes,
Children riding on red trikes,
New school clothes and bedtime kisses;
I served my sentence, thinking bliss is
This, it's all that I will get;
Submerged in womanhood, and yet
Asleep inside me, scarce a memory
Was this man, whose name was Emery.
I am not sure what set him free -
What chains or bars fell off of me -
One winter's day quite instantly -
I finally knew that I was ME.
So loved and welcome was this self -
So yearned for, recognized and held -
So whole and finished, able to live -
This is my spirit; it's all I can give.

# IS THE JOURNEY WORTH THE PAIN?
## Barbara Lantz

*I've been a single mother for fifteen years, and dealt with my child's issues alone until last year when I entered my first lesbian relationship. I'm 47, live in Seattle, and am a Health Information Manager in a not-for-profit community mental health center that provides both outpatient and inpatient services.*

What mother hasn't dreamed of having a little girl? When my daughter, Jenny, was born my dream came true -- I had my little girl. In a favorite picture of her, she is wearing a blue flowered dress with lace and a full petti-coat. She is laughing happily. She looked like my perfect dream. But there is a football helmet on her head.

As time went on, the billowy dresses and flowers disappeared. Instead, Jenny dressed herself in baseball gear and overalls. She climbed fences and couldn't be found where she was supposed to be. She was loud, energetic and loved rough and tumble games. She made me shake my head and say "I have a tomboy." O.K., many mothers have tomboys and love them dearly, right?

By mid-adolescence it was clear that Jenny was more than a tomboy. As a 16-year-old "dyke," she was so extreme in appearance that her role model was James Dean. She couldn't use public restrooms without someone calling security. The college kids in the apartment upstairs urinated on her bedroom window. The world was actively discriminating against her. There is no favorite picture from these years. Jenny had forgotten how to smile. There was no question that something needed to change so Jenny could have space to navigate in the world.

Jenny was more than a tomboy. Jenny told me she was a boy, or at least, she wanted to be one. Or to say it more clearly, she was a boy, but nature (did I do this?!) didn't get it right. Isn't that every mother's fear? -- that our children would not have

7

what they needed to survive? It was my fear, my struggle, my nightmare and my rebirth.

When I admitted these thoughts, I fell down the proverbial rabbit's hole. In 1995, my child was 19 and struggling to go to school, work part-time and deal with the emotional impact of admitting to himself and me that he was a female-to-male trans-gendered person. I lost my dreams of what a daughter could be.

I was raised in a strong matriarchal family and am proud of being a woman. There was a sense of betrayal -- my daughter didn't want to be my daughter. We shared a middle name with my mother. I would never have biological grandchildren to share that tradition. What would happen to the table that had been passed down from oldest daughter to oldest daughter for seven generations? What would I do with childhood pictures? How could I reconcile Jenny and the soon-to-be Daniel as being the same person? What about pronouns? My first reaction was "NO -- this is NOT going to happen -- not in my lifetime!"

Fortunately for us, Daniel stepped back and gave me time to think. After mulling the issue over, my biggest fear was that being transgendered meant that my child would never have a life with a partner, children, and a successful career. Fortunately, I was able to attend a national Female-to-Male conference held in Seattle. Most of the people I met there were established with careers and relationships. I started to believe there was a future for my child. I loved my child but still couldn't imagine what the end of this journey would look like or how I would manage it. One sensitive man from British Columbia sensed my confusion; he came up to me and assured me that he had been watching my child and was sure he would make a successful transition to being a man.

At 20, Daniel dropped out of college and lived in the world for a year as a man. His counseling had been successfully completed. The next stage became the central point of my hardest struggle -- because my child was so young I felt actively needed to help provide the much needed new chance at life. I asked him not to start his physical changes until he was 21. The time Daniel gave me by respecting my request was what I needed to intellectually accept the physical changes that were going to happen. At 21, he started taking hormones. In December 1997, I took Daniel to the hospital for his surgery and was in the recovery room with him.

I learned the details of hormones and cleaned the surgery incisions. I noticed the pimples as his beard came in and rubbed his muscles when they cramped from growing. I shared the additional expenses as he outgrew his clothes and boots and had to replace them. There was no place to hide and no way to escape.

I lost my ease in dealing with society. Preparations for my oldest son, Aaron's, wedding were agonizing. People who knew only Jenny had to be told about Daniel. We had to deal with their father's anger and frustrations, "Can't he be a girl this one time?" Aaron, a biological male, identified potential trouble makers and recruited his friends to be ready to evict guests if they mistreated Daniel. My daughter-in-law spent hours on the seating plan to try to keep Daniel and myself buffered by safe people.

I lost part of my family. One of my brothers no longer lets me be alone with my niece because of the "freak" I raised. Other family members just disappeared when we said, "You have to call him by his new name, 'Daniel.' "

I lost my sense of self. I discovered prejudice and hypocrisy within me. I thought a good parent was totally accepting all the time. I didn't like discovering I had selfish parts that didn't want what was best for my child. There was incredible anger towards Daniel: "I have to deal with this or that situation because of you." I didn't want to give up my dream daughter. I didn't want to learn that gender has a wide range of expressions and is more than male and female. Guilt threatened to immobilize me.

Over time, Daniel connected with successful trans-gendered men who became mentors. They helped educate him on legal and "passing" issues and the search for the right doctors. Spencer Bergstedt and Jason Cromwell showed Daniel ways to be a man without being a biological male. Aaron taught Daniel what he needed to know from the perspective of a biological male.

In addition, I have found a partner who knows Daniel is transgendered but has never known him as Jenny. Seeing my son through her eyes and the eyes of her children reinforces the understanding that Daniel's decision to start this process early in his life was the right one. The ability that Jean, my partner, has given me to see Daniel as an integrated person, plus the space our

9

male friends and Aaron have created, have allowed me to deal with the emotional impact of all these changes.

Because Daniel was so young, I got to see the changes on an everyday basis and was able to witness the incredible joy the changes were bringing him. I believe that the transition has been easier for both of us than if he had been an adult child because Daniel never lived in the world as a woman -- there was not much to unlearn. This has become the central point of some of my greatest joys.

What are the results of this journey? I gained an incredibly, sensitive and caring son who is comfortable with himself. (The down side is that we can't go out in public without someone flirting with him.)

There is great growth in knowing that gender is fluid and people can decide for themselves what traits they want to include as part of their most intimate self. If my partner were to die, I might search for a transgendered person because the ones I've met have internalized the parts of female and male that I most respect in individuals.

Freedom. Daniel and I can go out in public easily now. It used to be that we could go out to dinner or the movies but never both together because he couldn't use public restrooms. Last month we went out to a movie and dinner the same evening for the first time in five years.

As I integrate the pain and grief of my losses into the new person I'm becoming, I have a stronger sense of myself and my own worth. I see discrimination that has always existed but that I was too insulated to recognize. I'm Co-chair of the Cultural Diversity Committee at work because I have found a way and place to effect a change.

I have gained a new respect for my older son, his wife and my parents; they have completely accepted Daniel. My partner and her daughters have created a safe home where every one can be who they were meant to be.

We laugh. Aaron, a computer person, tells people his brother's "software was installed in the wrong hard drive" and is finally being put in the right box. I tell people my son had surgery for a birth defect that couldn't be corrected until he was an adult.

10

The family snickers every time I repeat this to "outsiders." My mother, who has Alzheimer's, called Jenny "Daniel," the name of her deceased brother for several years before Daniel started talking about being a man. She recently told her doctor that there was nothing wrong with her mind. She knew before anyone that Daniel was just like her brother Edwin.

There is a sense of peace now because of the love which is expressed in many different ways. Daniel never corrects his grandmother when she says Jenny because he knows she meant to say "Daniel." Daniel is patient in educating me and letting me ask questions. We count new facial hairs and are delighted with the heavy hair on his stomach and legs. He can now go swimming. He's comfortable with his body and has swimming trunks Jean gave him to celebrate his chest surgery. Dan calls his brother to ask , "Can I punch out the guy who cuts me off in traffic?" "What do I do with a tuxedo handkerchief?" "Can I sit down in the men's rest room?" He has started getting calls from women who want to go out with him, and yes, they know he's transgendered.

And what of the questions I had? I found the answers. Daniel modified his middle name from Elaine to Lain. He will still inherit the table -- he was the oldest daughter. Learning that gender bends and is flexible has helped redefine what really matters in a person. I have gained the ability to use the right pronoun when I'm talking about past, present and future events. I can get angry with the situation and not blame the person. I hope that science eventually finds a way to identify this as a birth defect so people starting the process can have financial assistance while transitioning.

I lost the dreams of a daughter but have gained dreams of a son. And I have discovered that I will always be a mother -- the dreams are for me alone. Do you think maybe Daniel will find a nice woman with a little girl I can spoil and love? There is a new favorite picture. Daniel is wearing a black tuxedo with a forest green vest. His white shirt shows how dark his hair and eyes are. He is laughing happily.

Like Alice in Wonderland, I have learned no matter how things change they also remain the same. You have to start a journey before it can end.

# YOU NEVER HAD A DAUGHTER
## Susan Bennett

*I have a background in journalism and public relations, but have recently worked as a fundraiser, currently at a continuing care retirement community. This has given me a great respect for the wisdom of the elderly. Besides Beecie, my first born, I also have a 15-year-old son, who is quite pleased to have a big brother. I enjoy horseback riding, reading, gardening and water sports.*

From the start, Beecie was clearly different from other little girls. She preferred overalls to dresses. She liked her hair short, with no ribbons, bows or hairclips. She was fascinated by male toy action figures, especially those that came equipped with weapons. She wore superman pajamas at night, an astronaut costume at Halloween, and a Fisher Price tool belt on Saturdays as she followed her father around the house.

During this stage, Beecie's differences didn't seem to matter -- to her or anyone else. She was simply a tomboy -- a girl who refused to let herself be defined by society's expectations, and I was proud of her. Yet at times, I wondered about my child. On Beecie's third birthday, I laid out an outfit of shorts and a matching shirt with ruffles. BC (the name my child uses today) says this day is one of his most vivid childhood memories. He recalls begging me to let him wear something else, to no avail. I vaguely recall asking Beecie why she didn't like the outfit, and being only momentarily confused by her unhappy answer: "I want to be a boy."

When Beecie started school, her kindergarten teacher commented, "Beecie plays roughly with the puppets. She makes them fight with one another." The comment didn't surprise me. But it did make me realize how "male" Beecie's behavior seemed to others. I am certain the teacher would not have made the comment had Beecie been a genetic boy.

In first grade, Beecie refused to take off her sweater after recess one day even though she was hot and flushed from playing outdoors. After some probing, the teacher learned the reason for Beecie's stubbornness: the front of her shirt had a huge pink appliquéd flower on it, and Beecie did not want anyone to see it.

After this incident, I tried to be more sensitive to Beecie's clothing preferences. She hated to shop, but when she did agree to go, she headed straight to the boys' department. I winced every time, and dreamt of the day my daughter and I would enjoy real shopping trips together.

Beecie's third grade school picture is one of my favorites. She is, untypically, wearing a gray cotton jumper printed with tiny pink flowers and a white blouse with a ruffled collar. I have no idea how I got her to wear it that day. But there she is, her sweet, freckled face smiling into the camera, the picture of a perfect, happy little girl. As she grew older, I began to realize what an aberration that picture was. And yet, I still look at it sometimes and wonder where that little girl went.

When Beecie was in fourth grade, she made a valiant attempt to be like the other girls. The New Kids on the Block were the rage, and Beecie wore New Kids T-shirts, bought New Kids tapes, and plastered New Kids posters on her bedroom wall with the best of them. Later, she would tell me that she never liked the New Kids, and was just trying to fit in.

Then, Beecie got a skater hair cut -- parted to the side, short on one side, longer on the other and shaved up the back. It was definitely a boy cut, and she was proud of it.

So far, the other kids had taken Beecie's individuality in stride. She had always been different, but they seemed to accept her without question. In fifth grade, that changed when she attended a new school. One night, I came into her room to find her lying on her bed, face to the wall. When I asked her what was wrong, she began to cry -- something she almost never did. At lunch that day, she had been rejected by a group of girls when she tried to sit with them. "Who asked you?!" they had demanded cruelly.

Another night, Beecie came into the kitchen while I was preparing dinner and told me her chest hurt. I asked her to show me where. She put her hands to her breasts, where two small knots were beginning to form. "Beecie," I said, "those are your breasts!" Her face fell, and she looked grief-stricken. Later, she told me that as a child, she would stand naked in front of the mirror and look at her chest, dreading the day that she would have breasts.

During middle school, Beecie grew progressively sullen, angry, and belligerent. She had always been an intense, strong-willed child whose personality tended to dominate the household. But now she began to lash out, screaming at her stepfather; beating up unmercifully on her younger brother; and challenging me physically. She was obviously very unhappy, but I didn't know how to help her. She refused to see a therapist. Once or twice, she broke down and cried, saying she felt "all wrong" but didn't know what to do about it.

I knew adolescent girls were supposed to be moody and emotional, so I tried to believe it was just hormones. But deep inside, I worried, and with good cause. Later, BC would tell me that he was so tormented by ninth grade, he easily could have ended his life if not for his friend Christine, to whom he was able to express the growing fear that he was a freak.

It was during that year, BC later told me, that he knew for certain he was a male inside, but this feeling frightened and confused him. He thought he was crazy and the only person who had ever felt that way. In agony, he became severely depressed. Only his nightly phone conversations with Christine got him through.

Finally, to his great relief, BC learned that there was a name for the way he felt. On the Internet one night, he discovered the term "transsexual," and he knew there were others like him.

It was another six months before the "T-word" came into my life. One day, I came across a spiral notebook which he was using as a journal. There were writings about being a man, and across one page were the words, "I am a transsexual." I was horrified -- so much so that I kept this revelation to myself as I tried to make sense of what I had read.

Around this time, BC began to diet and exercise excessively, even showing signs of mild bulimia. It was time to seek professional help, and this time BC accepted my offer. I was on the phone with a prospective therapist when BC picked up another receiver and heard me say, "My daughter thinks she is a transsexual." I had not yet confronted him with my journal discovery, but now he came to me and said, "Mom, we have to talk."

BC and I sat up late that night. He described the growing awareness throughout his life of being male. He told me how tormented he had been in middle school, how hard he had tried to fit in, how terrifying it had been to feel so different and not understand why. He told me how, finally, he had confessed his fears to Christine and how she had listened and comforted him. He told me about desperately searching on the Internet for clues to what he was experiencing, and finally discovering that it had a name and that he was not alone.

As I listened, my heart wrenched at the terrible pain he described, and I silently thanked God for sending Christine to share his burden when I couldn't. BC said he had wanted to tell me before, but feared my reaction. "Well," I said, "it is hard for me to comprehend. I feel like I'm losing my daughter." To that, BC responded with a remark that I will never forget: "But Mom," he said calmly, "you never had a daughter."

When I thought about it, I knew he was right, and this has been my saving grace. For when I got over being horrified long enough to stop and think, I knew that his words made absolute perfect sense, given all that that had gone before during my child's life. It was as if I were finally getting an answer to the question that had been forming in my mind for years.

Eventually, we found a wonderful psychiatrist associated with a gender identity program at a nearby university. At our first visit, I put up a brave front, but he could apparently see the difficulty I was having accepting the situation. I will always be grateful to him for giving me something positive to hold onto at that moment. After listening to BC for a few minutes, he commented on the tremendous inner strength which BC seemed to possess. Then he turned to me and said, "You must be some kind of parent, because that's where this kind of strength comes from."

After a series of visits, he confirmed that BC showed all the classic signs of transsexualism. Since then, BC has seen him regularly, and he has been a kind, thoughtful and wise advisor, supporting BC through his final two years of high school.

During the last two years, BC has moved forward with growing courage and anticipation towards becoming the person he was meant to be. During this period, he came out slowly to selected friends, coworkers, teachers and school administrators. Every time, he has been met with kindness, interest and support. He started hormone injections during the spring of his senior year. At graduation, he wore men's clothing under his robe.

In his opening remarks at graduation, the principal said there were many things for which he would remember this class. Then he began to name students that he would especially remember and why. To my complete surprise, the first name to come out of his mouth was my child's: "I will remember BC -- and Lisa -- for their courage," he said to an audience of several thousand.

With that one remark, the principal gave BC and me both a precious gift. By acknowledging BC's courage, the principal took my child's greatest struggle and publicly granted to it a sense of dignity and respect that I will remember and appreciate for the rest of my life.

### Update
The whole family has continued to be accepting and supportive. BC is in his third year of college and is happy and thriving. He works out regularly, eats incredibly healthfully, and just looks like a regular, cute guy who's enjoying life.


\* \* \* \* \*


To Create one's own world takes courage. Georgia O'Keefe (Jackie Greer)

# THE CHAMELEON
## Kay Morgan*

*I am a writer and mental health professional living in the San Francisco Bay Area with my partner and our two children, Wesley and a 4-year-old daughter (who sometimes claims to be a boy)!*

There used to be an axiom in the gay community that you could tell a person's sexual orientation by the way they walked. That might not work with Wesley. When he is wearing his boy clothes -- T-shirt, casual trousers, running shoes -- he walks with a bouncing strut. When he is dressed in his feminine clothes -- "girl attitude" blouse and long, flowing skirt -- he swishes his hips, even holds up one limp wrist.

Wesley was always different. Artistic. Charming. Verbal. Analytical. Adored by women. A compliant little boy with infinite concentration.

Boy play? Trucks and trains? Ball games, bike riding? Absolutely no interest. He wouldn't even pretend. He marched to his own drummer, thank you just the same.

Boy clothes? As soon as he could talk, he made it clear that he was not going to wear blue jeans or other butch clothes. No way. When he was 4, he wanted to dress up in beautiful outfits. We bought him an elegant shawl. He wore it around the house. We took him to a G-rated drag show at the local gay bar. He was entranced. He wanted to go every week. He wore his shawl there. The show's leather-clad host had Wesley stand up and show the audience his stuff. (Wesley still loves drag. Unfortunately, where we now live it is hard to find drag shows that are suitable for children, and the Pride Parade comes only once a year.)

As he entered elementary school, he evolved a chameleon-like ability to mask his differentness. Perhaps he learned a lesson from the Pokemon shoes incident. He had insisted on buying the beautiful pink shoes, despite our warning that they might cause teasing. Sure enough, a boy in his kindergarten class ridiculed them as "girl shoes." He never wore the shoes again, and from then on he has checked with us to make sure his school clothes were made for boys.

My partner and I talked about how to approach Wesley's uniqueness. We assured him that it was other people, not he, that were sometimes narrow-minded. That in some parts of the world, boys and men could wear makeup and dress colorfully. And that he could be himself around us.

At age 9, his gender ambiguity is very apparent, when he chooses to reveal himself. His self-assurance is also apparent. A classmate's mom described him as extraordinarily self-assured. "He knows who he is," she said admiringly.

At school, he dresses in the typical boys' manner. Nothing fancy or butch, just casual slacks, shirts, and running shoes. Perhaps a baseball cap in the summer. Carefully chosen boxer shorts underneath. He can even mimic the strut of the popular gangsta style if he so chooses.

A close look reveals that he has managed to smuggle in some of his accouterments. Nothing too obvious. Just a low-key necklace and a ring. He cautiously tested out these adornments and found that while one or two kids teased him, at least an equal number -- both boys and girls -- complimented him.

At home these days, he lets it all hang out. A gorgeous flowing skirt with butterflies. A colorful blouse with a tag labeled "Girl Power."

Like everything with Wesley, the gender bending began cautiously. He donned one of my partner's old slips, pinned to fit his narrow waist. He began wearing the slip to bed every night. When it broke, he asked if he could buy a new one. In the girl's section of the department store he was timid, not wanting anyone to see him. He said he was buying it for his "sister." When I went along with his charade, saying, "Yeah, your twin sister," his eyes expressed gratitude, and he threw his arm around me.

What to do when our parents visit? We give Wesley the message that he can be whoever he wants to be. Yet, we know our own parents (both sets) will frown on us if we "allow" him to be too feminine.

I gave him a subtle warning. "You can dress however you

18

want to when your grandma is here. But she's kind of old-fashioned, and she may say something if she sees you in that skirt."

"Like what?" he asks. I wonder if his naïveté is feigned, or real. "Like, 'Those are girl clothes!' "

He decides to test her, like he tested his schoolmates by wearing jewelry. He prances into the livingroom in his girl outfit, swishing his hips. My partner and I subtly stiffen in anticipation. His grandma's initial reaction is, "How gorgeous!" Then, she does a double-take. "What is that you are wearing?" she asks incredulously.

He continued to wear his favorite outfit for the remainder of his grandmother's trip. She may have had more thoughts on the topic, but she did not voice them.

My father might be less tolerant. He would not say anything directly to Wesley. Instead, I can imagine him taking me outside and lecturing me on the perils of manhood.

Some of our lesbian friends might even privately raise their eyebrows. Encouraging stereotypically male behaviors in their own sons, they no more understand or support Wesley's gender sensibilities than does the heterosexual mainstream.

It's hard not to be self-conscious, to feel that people will blame us for Wesley's differentness. That they will think we are encouraging it. That, not being men, we fail to realize the level of condemnation that can be heaped upon a boy who is not masculine. That it's all because he has no father to set him straight.

Of course I worry about Wesley. He seems so fragile. What will the world do to him because he is different? What will happen to him in the perilous junior high school years?

But I also have tremendous pride in him. His centeredness and self-confidence are so amazing. I love his radiant personality that draws people to him, and may shelter him from malevolence.

A lesbian friend describes him as the most "perfectly androgynous" person she has ever met.

Research suggests that children of lesbian parents tend to be less gender-stereotyped than children of heterosexual parents. That is, the girls are a little less feminine and more interested in nontraditional careers, and the boys are a little less masculine and more emotionally expressive. I wonder how many more boys would be like Wesley if their parents felt empowered to let them circumvent society's straight-jacketing. And wouldn't that be an interesting world?

So, not only am I proud of Wesley, but I am also proud of us, his parents, for giving him the room to blossom so beautifully. And I am proud to be a member of a larger community that provides space for him to be himself.

***

### Secret Identity
Veronica West

Trying to live
two lives crammed into the time allotted
for one.
By day, I play
the role of the good husband,
faithful to a fault.

I live
as my other self
in stolen moments
when you are away.

Only then can I drop
the veil
and show my true
face.

I feel
like Clark Kent
ducking into a phone booth
to emerge
as Wonder Woman.

# MUSCLE MAN
## Kate McAdow

*I am a former counselor and literature teacher who began writing for young adults five years ago. My second novel tells the story of a gentle boy much like my own son and other boys my husband and I have met in our three years of meeting with families with gender-atypical children. My husband administers an animal welfare organization and my adult daughter is an attorney.*

My strong, muscular, eight-year-old boy with gorgeous thighs, thicker than my hands can span, so coordinated at two and a half he could hit a baseball. A boy full of jokes, guffaws, shouts, daredevil rock climbing, leaping, squirming, teasing, tickling, swearing, wrestling. How can he want to play dress-up in my slips and his sister's old dresses? It's inconceivable ... it's baffling ... it's disastrous.

When Michael was two and a half, every noun took a "she," never a "he." A dog was "she," a cat "she," a butterfly, a fox, all "she." We assumed he'd learn, and he did.

He had an eye for pretty things. Standing in line, I'd hear his tiny voice addressing the woman behind me -- "I like your skirt/your shoes/your hair/your dress."

"What a sweet boy! You've made my day!"

Few of us notice the efforts our elders make to muster energy enough to maintain their dignity, but my three-year-old noticed. The memory of his understanding of my elderly parents' struggle in the face of decay, brings a lump to my throat. His simple untutored eye sees beauty, and speaks it.

Textures, especially the smooth and shiny, delight him. Vivid colors paint his world. Everywhere there is beauty he needs to show us -- a shaft of wheat, misty spider-webs glistening in morning sun, the red jolt of a cardinal, the pleasure of a blue jay.

Michael liked to play dress-up, as his older sister had long before he was born. I hate high heels myself, and our life is casual, so he rarely saw me primp or fondle fancy dresses. Those rare occasions thrilled him. On Halloween, at age three, he wanted to wear his sister's old ballet tutu. Other kids cross-dress at Halloween, so we had no objection. But he never wanted to take the thing off. We were seeing, too, how important female images were. Watching movies, he was only interested in Wendy and Tinker Bell and Ariel, not Mowgli or Prince Arthur. Care Bears and ponies, not Ninja Turtles or Power Rangers. At the video store, age eight and a half, he chooses The Swan Princess.

Trying to keep the communication lines open, we inquire and learn that he wants to be a girl. Why? "The dolls -- they have long hair." What does he like about long hair? He can't put it into words; he just likes it. He accepts himself, for now, and a child psychologist concurs. Michael likes his body, and peeing standing up.

Michael's dad works at home. No commute, lots of time to play, wrestle, bike together, swim, go to the park. But Michael has zero interest in balls, bats, or gloves. At the park and at school he gets along with kids, especially the chatty ones.

When he begins to receive an allowance, he saves it for 10 or 12 weeks, then buys himself dolls -- Barbies or cheaper substitutes. When a girl comes over to play, she brings her Barbies. When a boy comes over, Michael says the dolls here belong to his big sister. He and the boys swim, bike, build a tree house, or dig up rocks to trade. We've persuaded him to try soccer and t-ball. Now, given the choice of a sport, he's picked gymnastics.

Gradually, over the years, he's learned from peers that it's not cool to comment on the natural world except for the odious or titillating. But when he walks alone on a rainy day, he patiently stoops to rescue worms lingering in the road. Then he comes home, flops down with crayons and paper, and draws -- red-haired mermaids -- purple and orange angelfish -- black whales -- yellow crabs.

At age seven, he began to ask about the mysteries -- death, God, birth. We talked about what may happen after death, musing on what we'd like to be in our next lifetime. I say, "a bird -- a heron, or maybe an eagle." Michael says, "I hope next time I'm born a girl."

## UPDATE

Now 15 and a ninth-grader, Michael has yet to declare his sexual orientation. My husband and I try to include gay-positive comments when we talk of people and lifestyles. At high school he is sometimes teased by a couple of boys because he talks mostly to girls. Last week he was told that his blue backpack is purple, and purple is a 'gay' color. He's taking karate, and seems more confident that he could defend himself physically if necessary. We hope that in art classes next year he will meet more boys who share his interests.

Michael knows that the support group we attend is for parents of kids with gender-atypical interests. He has met other kids in the group, and enjoys talking, playing games, and drawing with them, even showing them his drawings of super-heroines.

But he is ambivalent. After showering a friend with gifts on Valentine's Day, he told us, "I'm glad I have a crush on a girl, because it means I'm not gay. I don't want to be gay."

Do not go where the path may lead, go instead where there is no path, and leave a trail. Ralph Waldo Emerson. (MMB)

# TELL GRANDMA I'M A BOY
## Florence Dillon*

*My children, husband and I live with a golden retriever (male), a cat (female), and a cockatiel (gender indeterminate). Working to make the elementary school environment safe for our son has convinced me that public awareness of the realities of transgendered experience is critical for the healthy development and survival to adulthood of all gender-variant children.*

My husband and I have two sons.  Like most siblings, they're enmeshed in a love-hate relationship as rivals at home; they staunchly defend each other in the world outside.  Alex, who just turned fourteen, is a classical musician and computer whiz. He's wired his room like a space station command center. He seems to have weathered puberty with ease, his voice is deeper, his personality composed.

Steve just turned eleven.  His life revolves around rocketry, soccer, and improvising stand-up comedy routines in the kitchen.  Still enjoying the comfortable androgyny of childhood, he's in denial about puberty being just around the corner.  As his parents, we're concerned about the changes puberty will bring, because we know how distressing it will be for him to begin to develop breasts in middle school.  And we're sure that, unless something is done to postpone or stop it, he will develop breasts and begin to menstruate, because this child, who feels and behaves in every way like an ordinary boy, has a normal female body.

When our second child was born, the doctor lifted the tiny, squirming baby so my husband, James, could see it clearly.  I heard jubilation in James' voice as he announced, "It's Sarah!" That was the name we had decided to give our first baby girl.  By the time we left the hospital 24 hours later, our daughter's birth certificate read "Sarah Elizabeth Anne," honoring both her grandmothers.

During her first year of life, Sarah ate, slept, and watched the world through wide, wise eyes. An avid breast-feeder, she was almost never out of my arms, and almost never made a sound. This observant stillness erupted into a storm of vigorous activity shortly after age one, however, accompanied by a torrent of grammatically complex sentences.

Her father and I were delighted with her verbal skills but terrified by her tendency to seek out the most hazardous physical challenges. Our experience with her more cautious older brother, Alex, hadn't prepared us for this toddler who would climb to the top of anything with handholds and, later, the preschooler who loved to jump from the tallest branch of our backyard tree down to the roof of the garage. But we were very proud of this child. I had always wanted a daughter who would define herself, who would grow to be strong and intelligent and independent. As a girl, I had been surrounded by capable women living purposeful lives, my mother and grandmothers and aunts, who loved me and made me feel very happy to be female. I grew up believing I could be and do whatever in the world I wanted, and one of the things I wanted most was to be a mother. Birthing this lively, fierce, and thoughtful little girl gave me a chance to hand down the powerful woman-centered heritage that had cradled me. I wanted to create a safe, warm nest where I could mother my daughter, then set her free to fly.

Sarah tested my resolve to set her free in a way I had never imagined. On her third birthday, she tore the wrapping paper from one of her grandmother's gifts and discovered a pink velvet dress trimmed in ribbons and white lace. I knew she wouldn't want to wear it. She hadn't voluntarily put on anything but pants since turning two, and this dress was totally impractical for playing the way Sarah played. Nevertheless, I was surprised by her reaction. She looked up, not unhappy, but puzzled and confused, and asked,"Why is Grandma giving me a dress? Doesn't she know I'm not the kind of girl who wears dresses?" Then, with an air of great satisfaction at finding the solution to her problem, she added, "Just tell Grandma I'm a boy." Initially, I assumed Sarah's announcement was simply an attempt to communicate a clothing preference in language she thought grownups would understand.

Then, a few weeks later, Sarah said she wanted us to call her "Steve." We thought this an odd but harmless request, and tried to remember to say "Steve" from time to time. Then we received a call from the Sunday school teacher who taught the three-year-olds at our church. She told us Sarah had asked her to cross out "Sarah" and write "Steve" on her name tag. We realized from this that the name "Steve" must be very important to Sarah, so we told the teacher it would be all right to call her "Steve" for the time being. At home, we talked to Sarah about the difference between a nickname like" Steve" and her real name. But in our neighborhood and on the playground at the park, Sarah began to introduce herself only as Steve. Within our family, she became more insistent that she was a boy. She never said "I want to be a boy" or "I wish I were a boy," but always, "I am a boy." She demanded we use masculine pronouns when referring to her. When we forgot or refused, her face would screw up in fury and exasperation, and the offending parent was likely to be pinched or kicked by this usually loving child. I stopped using pronouns altogether when Sarah was within earshot.

The teacher at our Montessori preschool wasn't as flexible as the Sunday school teacher. The children were learning to write their names, and "Sarah" was evidently the only name the teacher was willing to teach. This became an issue as Christmas approached. Four-year-old Sarah came home one day and asked how to spell "Steve" so she could sign her letter to Santa. When I cautioned that Santa might not be able to find our house if the name on the letter wasn't correct, she looked at me scornfully. "Santa knows where I live, Mommy. He knows my name is Steve."

I decided it was time to seek professional help. I had no idea why Sarah was convinced it was better to be a boy. Surely someone could tell me what I was doing wrong. And it must be something I was doing, or failing to do, because the children were in my care twenty-four hours a day. No one else had as many opportunities to influence them. My husband was successfully pursuing a corporate career that required his attention eleven or twelve hours a day, and I, very much by choice after fifteen years of work and academia, was a full-time mom. Our single-earner lifestyle, unusual in the 1990's, fulfilled the nostalgic fantasy of nuclear family life in the 1950's. I baked whole-wheat bread, cooked organically-grown vegetables, read aloud to my children every day, and volunteered in Alex's first-grade classroom two mornings each week when Sarah was in preschool.

My first call for help was to our state university's human development department. When I described my child and our family's situation, the "human development specialist" who took the call laughed reassuringly and said, "Don't worry about a thing. Your child has a great imagination. Lots of bright, creative kids try out different roles at this age. She'll grow out of it." With relief, I took her advice, stopped worrying, and waited for her to grow out of it. For the next couple of years, I supported my child's wish to be called Steve. I no longer made her unhappy by insisting, "You're a girl." Instead I said, "You have a girl's body, though Mommy and Daddy know you feel like a boy."

But I still felt responsible for my second child's not being able to accept that she was a girl, and set out to correct whatever misapprehensions she might have about becoming a woman. Because being a mother was such a joy for me, I told Sarah that what was wonderful about being a girl is that girls can grow up and have babies of their own. Hearing this, Sarah's face darkened. She shuddered and said, "I don't want to talk about that." She asked if everyone had to get married and have babies when they grew up.

When told no, of course not, she relaxed and said she was always going to live in our house with Alex.

By age five, Sarah had given all her dresses to a neighbor girl of the same age who loved dressing up. She wouldn't put on any item of clothing without first asking if it was made for a boy or a girl. Only boys' clothes would do. For Sarah, having an older brother ensured plenty of boys' hand-me-downs. That saved me the discomfort of shopping often for my daughter in the boys' departments of clothing stores. Even when Sarah wasn't with me, I felt compelled to confess to sales clerks that I was buying these shirts and pants and sport coats for my daughter who evidently thought it was better to be a boy. For some reason, I believed I owed perfect strangers an explanation of something I couldn't explain to myself.

27

Since traditional feminine dress and behavioral expectations were so distasteful to Sarah, I began a campaign to separate these "cultural trappings" from the biological fact of being female. I wanted Sarah to know she could be whatever kind of woman she wanted to be; she had the right to define herself as a person without regard to anyone else's expectations. Not only did she not have to get married and have children, but she would never have to put on a dress or makeup or wear her hair in any particular style unless she wanted to. She could pursue any kind of work she wanted. She could continue to be physically active and competitive all her life. I looked for children's books with strong female protagonists. Not at all athletic myself, I made friends with active, "outdoorsy" women who could be better role models than I for this sports-minded kid. Whenever a woman was mentioned in the news for any type of achievement, I trumpeted it loudly for Sarah's ears. To encourage our child to develop a well-rounded self-image, James would tell Sarah how pretty she was at the same time we were congratulating her on her strength and intelligence. We had read some-where that the most successful professional women remember their fathers' recognizing and valuing their attractiveness as well as their intellectual accomplish-ments.

One day, after years of exposure to our "women can do anything" message, my seven-year-old turned to me with tearful eyes and said, "Mommy, you only like girls." Suddenly, I realized that everything I'd been doing to help my child feel good about herself had instead made him feel that I didn't accept or love who he really was. My child was Steve, a wonderfully creative, articulate, and very patient boy who had been waiting his whole life for his parents to see him.

Today, Steve is known as a boy by his classmates. He is serving as president of the fifth grade and holds school records for push-ups and sit-ups. A very supportive administrator solved the classic bathroom problem by establishing single-person rest rooms for Steve's class. Instead of labeling them "boys" and "girls," there is one for "kids" and one for "adults." The principal of the middle school Steve will attend next year has agreed to list him as a boy on all school documents. I'm writing this under a pseudonym to protect his privacy.

So we've come to the brink of puberty, when the disconnect between biology and gender threatens the psychological health Steve has so buoyantly maintained since his family acknowledged his reality and began to advocate for him in the world at large. It has been more than eight years since our three-year-old first said, "Just tell Grandma I'm a boy." That message has never varied.

We've learned to listen to our child. He's the only expert on his own experience. And, although his parents and older brother find it helpful to describe him as transgendered, Steve doesn't refer to himself that way. As far as Steve is concerned, he is simply a boy.

## UPDATE

Steve is now 15, living the typical life of an adolescent male (although he's practicing very safe sex). He finished ninth grade with straight "A"s. But he had fun, too, and continues to be popular with both boys and girls. None of this would have been possible if he had not felt accepted as a boy.

Sensitive, supportive administrators and teachers have allowed him to be himslf in both middle school and high school. We're working with a pediatric endocrinologist to help him avoid female puberty and to make it easier for him, ultimately, to live as a man.

Steve is good-looking, witty and intelligent. He is writing songs for the acoustic guitar and perfecting his tennis game. At the moment, he plans to be an architect, a journalist or a professional skate boarder. We are very proud of our son.

# PFLAG and the TRANSGENDER NETWORK

Perhaps the greatest help in our personal journey has been PFLAG--both the support we found there, and also that organization's willingness to embrace the trans community. Soon after our own son came out as an FtM transsexual we found that PFLAG's mission did not include transgendered people, so we set about to correct that.

Following a transgender workshop at the 1995 national conference, we found a half dozen people interested in providing a trans presence within PFLAG. Soon an email list was developed and grew to about 100 participants within a month or two. Our group was first known as TSON, but later shortened to TNET.

With Jessica Xavier as chief author, the little 14 page booklet, *Our Trans Children*, was developed and became a key piece in educating PFLAG chapters. It has sold over 40,000 copies to PFLAG chapters, universities, families, practitioners and more. An excellent introduction to trans issues, its 4th expanded edition is due in the spring of 2003.

We found growing support in PFLAG for adding "gender identity" to the national by-laws, which was made official in September 1998. More recently, a Board resolution was passed to support only legislation that includes ALL our GLBT family. PFLAG was the first national gay-related organization to make both such courageous moves, and for that we are ever grateful.

Over 250 PFLAG chapters have identified Transgender Coordinators who are responsible for educating their chapters, welcoming trans persons and their families and working with area trans groups. We also need trans-gendered persons around the country to visit their local PFLAG chapters and to help educate these loving families.

Karen Gross, also the mother of an adult FtM, runs TNET's Help Line and several email lists. Contact her at (216) 691-HELP (4357), or email: IMATMom@aol.com.

For information on ordering our booklet, *Our Trans Children*, or about contacting your local PFLAG chapter, please contact this editor; see information on the last page.

# PART II

# LEARNING FROM OUR

# ADULT CHILDREN

# THE JOURNEY BEGINS
## Karen and Bob Gross

*Karen and Bob reside in Cleveland Ohio. Karen taught elementary school and now is a postpartum doula, caring for mothers and new-born babies. Bob is a CPA. They have two children, one whom you will read about, and one who is a pediatrician. Karen and Bob are active in the LGBT community. In 2002, they were grand marshals in the Cleveland Gay Pride Parade.*

I always wanted a daughter and was finally taking Michelle home from the hospital! She was pretty, bright, and a very good baby until I brought her brother home from the hospital when Michelle was two.

Michelle went into the "terrible twos" and stayed there for a long time. A loner, by the time she was six it was almost impossible to get her to dress in any way feminine. Dresses, dolls, and long hair were out; her brother's underwear, boys' shirts, short hair, and doing boy things were in. We took her to a child psychologist; we were told to save our money. "Your child is not into alcoholor drugs, is a good student, and wasn't complaining anyway, so just save your money."

Michelle became defensive, quick to anger, and was probably very depressed through most of school. She was, however an excellent student. At Ohio State University, she changed from engineering to psychology, graduated, got married, and began a dual Master of Social Work, Juris Doctor (law) program. Then one evening, she and her husband came to our house.

"We are getting a divorce," she said. "As you know, I have been in counseling at college for several years, and now I know who and what I really am. I will be starting male hormone therapy, my voice will deepen, I will grow facial hair, and I am taking on a new persona. From now on, call me 'Mitchell' and please watch the pronouns." I cried all night. Little did I know that while I was losing a daughter, I would soon gain a son and a new

33

hobby. I began to try to learn all I could about my child's gender identity problem.

My husband seemed to take it all in stride. "Maybe it's just a phase," he opined. "We'll just have to see what happens." As Mitch was becoming happier, less defensive, and showed a developing sense of humor, Bob began to talk more with him. Bob said that because of his science background, he knew that gender identity, like sexual orientation, had to be mostly hard wired and not a choice. What surprised me more was my parents' reaction and that of Bob's mother. There was never a question of their support for Mitch.

A newspaper account of a male paramedic who was "outed" for transitioning to female led me to contact her. Lunch followed, and we began to look for other transgendered people and their families to join us in the creation of a support group. Mitch went to a national conference on the West coast and came back home to announce that there were hundreds like him. My thirst for information led me to the Internet, email and to PFLAG (Parents, Families and Friends of Lesbians and Gays). Soon I was in touch with Mary Boenke, the mother of a transgendered son like Mitch. Soon after that Bob and I were traveling around the Midwest to tell our story, trying to make people aware of transgendered issues.

Our support group grew to a monthly meeting in our home that attracts 30 to 60 people each month. T-Folks, their parents, brothers and sisters, spouses and children, doctors, psychologists, and clergy have attended. An online email support group soon grew into six different groups, each with its own special interests. These email support groups can be found on our web site at www.transfamily.org. I have had a lot of help along the way. I learned quickly that the best way to help yourself is by helping others, and encouraging them, also, to help others.

## UPDATE

Meanwhile, Mitch has changed in many ways. He has had some surgery; he has grown a mustache and goatee. His orientation has not changed. He was, and is, attracted to men. (He tells us that he always self-identified as a gay guy in a woman's body.) He changed his name legally, changed his driver's license, but could

34

not change his Ohio birth certificate. He met a gay man, Charlie, who loved him for who he is. They decided to get married. They listened to the judge explain that two men could not be married in Ohio; that it depended on their birth certificates. When Mitch and Charlie showed their birth certificates, with one F and one M, the judge had to approve a marriage license. Thank you, Ohio!

We had a beautiful ceremony and celebration later at home, with parents and grandparents, friends and other family members participating. We are very proud of that LEGAL gay, transgendered, Jewish-Catholic wedding!

At this writing, they have been married three years. Mitch still kids about starting a support group for children whose parents are more out than they are. Our support group, TransFamily of Cleveland, has joined with the local Lesbian/Gay Center, GLSEN (Gay, Lesbian Stuents...), and PFLAG, all of which have become very supportive of transgender issues. Our groups participate in SAFE, Safe Schools Are For Everyone. We and other members of TransFamily speak to counselors, teachers, and graduate students at local high schools and colleges. All of this is to try to raise the awareness of the public to the issues facing transgendered people on a daily basis.

In today's society, some children are discarded for being different, much less transgendered. Many of our early fears were self-directed. How would our parents take the news? What would our friends say? We learned that parents and friends took their cues from us. If we were okay, they were okay. After all, it wasn't their problem. Although we no longer have a daughter, we have a much happier son. We are also pleased that many wonderful folks, whose families and friends abandoned them, are now a part of our own extended family.

***

Human Salvation lies in the hands of the creatively maladjusted.

I have decided to stick with Love. Hate is too great a burden to bear.
--both Martin Luther King, Jr. (Audette Fulbright)

# FROM ANGER TO ACCEPTANCE
## -- A MOTHERS STORY
### Barbara Lister

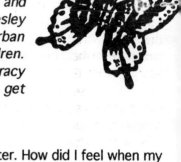

*I was born in 1913 in Boston, a beginning which shaped my standards and values. After graduation from Wellesley College I married James M. Lister, Urban Planner, and had five wonderful children. Later I began teaching adult literacy classes, have continued tutoring, and get my greatest satisfaction as a teacher.*

My son has become my daughter. How did I feel when my eldest son -- Swarthmore, Peace Corps, committed Christian -- announced to me that he felt unsuited to being a man and wished to enter the world of make-up and panty hose and live as a woman? How do I feel, three years later, when the gender change has been completed? This is the story of my journey from shocked outrage to acceptance.

Nothing in Michael's life had prepared me for such a revelation. He was the oldest son in our "normal" suburban family. My husband and I assumed that our five would grow up happy and well-adjusted in their busy life of school and Scouts, horses, and family togetherness. Michael was a rosy-checked, energetic toddler, a husky boyish youngster.

As an adolescent, Michael studied dutifully and was valedictorian of his class. He did not excel at sports but became a skillful bird-watcher. I recognized that he was shy and awkward around girls, but because I had suffered from a similar anxiety in the world of high school dating I thought it uncomfortable but natural. At Swarthmore he majored in Chemistry but had little interest in life in a lab. The opportunity to be a Peace Corps teacher in Malaysia was a peak experience. He liked teaching at an English- speaking boys' school, made good friends of both sexes, and savored the exotic sights and cultural diversity that is

Malaysia.

His re-entry into ordinary living was to him, as to many Peace Corps volunteers, a traumatic experience. One night a midnight call came to us from Michael, "Can you help me? I'm afraid I'll jump out of the window." The resulting depression was gradually alleviated by the healing care of a residential treatment program. Michael subsequently managed to weather a good many years in steady but unfulfilling jobs and a marriage that ended in divorce. Through it all he was aided by his Christian beliefs, which nourished him but added to his sense of guilt as he faced a scary Father God.

A second hospitalization for depression led him to move to Cleveland to stay with me, recently widowed. He found a new job in a travel agency. I felt that finally he was gaining confidence and new skills. Then one fateful morning he showed me a newspaper article about a successful Cleveland entertainer who had changed gender from man to woman. While I was scanning the article with slight interest, he plucked up his courage to say, "I showed you this because I want to become a woman."

I was horrified, that this 50-year-old son could con-template an action so bizarre and repugnant. Several days later, when I had cooled down somewhat, he gingerly suggested that I might want to meet someone who had made the change, perhaps invite that person to dinner so that we could talk. My answer, I am ashamed to say, was, "I don't think I could have such a person under my roof." We agreed to meet at a restaurant. "Chris" was waiting for us, well-dressed, feminine enough, self assured. During the dinner conversation, I learned that she had a successful freelance advertising business. Talking later with her mother, Mrs. H., made me feel less isolated and frightened. She had seen a depressed and unhappy son become a happy and coping new person. She assured me that a mother's acceptance is possible.

Still I poured out to my journal a tumult of feelings, usually accompanied by tears. Anger--why was he doing this to me? Fear--would he lose his job and have no future? Embarrassment -- how could I ever be seen in his company? I remember crying out bitterly to my journal, "I want to have a temper tantrum right in front of him so he will know what he is doing to me!"

I faced a dilemma. Having Michael live with me was a pleasant arrangement. Most importantly, his being there to help made it possible for me to remain in my home. I faced a bleak choice: either adapt to Michael's gender change or move into a retirement community.

At this point I had some help on the road to acceptance. I hesitantly confided in a kindly woman minister who said to me, "You love Michael, don't you? Then you have no choice." I joined a Grief Group at my church and Cleveland's well-established "Gender Program" enabled me to talk with a psychiatrist in Michael's presence.

His brothers and sisters were also struggling. The confrontation of the siblings at Christmas time was bitter and largely unforgiving. Over the months each gradually at his own pace accommodated to the change. However, it was not until a family reunion after the surgery that the structure of the family re-formed to include this new person whom they decided to christen with a more affectionate name, "Kelly."

Meanwhile, Michael, was going through the steps necessary to become Miquelle. In thrift shops he began to assemble a woman's wardrobe for the office. A friend who sold Avon products helped him with makeup. I went with him, embarrassed, of course, to choose a becoming wig. He tried dressing where he would not be recognized and also at the meetings of transsexuals and "cross dressers", who got together once a month for support and information. He had regular counseling under the Gender Program, and started the long, expensive process of electrolysis.

Another step involved writing all the members of the extended family, trying to explain to them that he was becoming the person he had always thought himself to be. Then there were the legal steps -- driver's license, bank account, Social Security, passport. The final hurdle was the job. Because his work did not require him to meet the public, the office gave him permission to work there as Miquelle. I watched in anguish as the new person set off to meet the test. How did she look? If you were critical you would focus on the man's hands, the size 13 shoes, the masculine bones of the face. If you loved her, you would focus on the graceful clothes, the face-softening hair style and make-up, the new radiance to the eyes.

When her job was phased out because of a merger, she was able to get a more responsible job in another travel agency where the workers knew her story but were ready to welcome her. Friends, both old and new, seemed to extend to her a deeper level of caring. A new personality was emerging -- more affectionate, more self-assured, and certainly happier.

Under the strict supervision of the Gender Board, and with continued counseling, Miquelle had begun taking female hormones after having lived for a year as a woman. Now she was judged ready for the surgery with a skillful plastic surgeon in Montreal. I balked at the idea of genital surgery, but when my daughter-in-law said she dreamed that my deceased husband appeared to her and said he was worried what Kelly might do if she did NOT have surgery, I decided to support her. I went with her for the first few days of hospitalization and contributed to the cost.

Being with her during that time made a profound impression on me. I learned that every week a new group of patients came from all over the country, even fundamentalist Christians, for sexual reassignment. Miquelle was not unique. I heard stories of pain and rejection. A surprising uniformity was in their reports. Most agreed that, when they were about five, when school began to separate girls and boys, each began to have the shameful certainty that he could not feel as other boys did. It was a guilty feeling which he dared not share with anyone. As he grew older he tried to hide it by "macho" acts like growing a beard. Perhaps he married and fathered children, hoping that the feelings would go away. Still he felt, as they all described it, like a woman "trapped in a man's body." The struggle to deny this feeling led usually to depression, often even to thoughts of suicide. I heard, too, of the joy of the new identity.

To accept these experiences, I did not need the confirmation given to the skeptical by recent researchers in the Netherlands. In comparing a small region of the hypothalamus, where the roots of sexuality are thought to live, these researchers discovered a significant difference in the size of this tiny structure in the brain of male-to-female transsexuals as compared with normal males. The report concluded, "This finding may cast light on the larger issue of sexual identity, of what makes a person feel comfortable -- or tormented -- as a man or woman."

Miquelle now says she feels herself to be wholly the person she was meant to be. As she said to me the other day, "Walking home tonight wearing a blouse and skirt, I realized a difference. I have worn skirts for several years, but I still knew part of my body was male. Now, I am no longer as concerned that my appearance be as feminine as possible so that no one will suspect my story. Now I feel real and genuine. I thank my Creator every day for allowing me to become a woman."

I have changed, too. When I began this parenting business I naively assumed that two competent parents plus a comfortable home would produce a series of "Dick and Jane" children who would go to the right colleges, get good jobs, and bring their children home for the holidays. My adult children, of course, have each had some difficult times, but Michael shattered my stereotype of what was acceptable. I had to learn that loving involves letting go. The child you love must follow his own path no matter how unlike the one you would have chosen for him. While learning this I have lost a son, it's true. But I have a new, most remarkable daughter.

## A Success Story

Two years later the memory of my anger has faded, as has the memory of that lost person, my eldest son, Michael. The new person, Kelly, has become familiar and loved. I have changed. too. As a token mother who is available to talk with any other troubled parents, I attend with Kelly a support group for Transgenders. I have come to feel respect and affection for all those who, because of their feeling of incongruity, are willing to face so much pain in order, as they say, "to have their bodies match the selves they are within."

# A LETTER TO ALLEN
## John Boenke

*I am the father of a transsexual son. I am retired from an engineering management career and have long been active in civil rights issues. I have been married for almost 44 years, have three wonderful children, and five beautiful grandchildren.*

Dear Allen:

I have been meaning to write this letter for some time. It is long overdue, but I needed to get my thoughts in order so that I may say all I want to say in the best possible way.

I don't remember your ever being much trouble. Even when you were born, your timing was very helpful. I took Mom to the hospital with your brother, older by two years, riding along. We dropped Mom at the hospital and continued into town to pick up your grandmother who was arriving at the bus station. She had agreed to come and help with the extra work necessitated by your arrival.

By the time I got back to the nursery, you had arrived and were there waiting for me, greeting me with a quiet or even, it might be called, a gracious smile. It was then I learned you were a little girl.

You were slow in learning to walk because of your infancy celiac disease. Luckily, it was finally diagnosed, and we learned to control the illnes through a limited diet, until you grew out of it. You wanted to walk but did not quite have the strength or ability. So, as soon as I got home from work, you would come crawling over and want me to help you. You would hold my fingers, and we would go round and round in the halls. You led, toddling in front with arms raised, holding onto my fingers, and I walked along behind, bent over and carefully trying to avoid stepping on you as we gyrated along.

Then, again, your timing was excellent. One afternoon Mom and I were sitting on the floor, sending you back and forth

41

between us. You would take one or two steps on your own, then collapse onto the floor or in our arms. Except once, you took a couple steps and kept going -- and have been going ever since. That same evening your little sister arrived. It was almost as though you had known it was time for you to move on.

You were the artist in the family, you were the dreamy one, the quiet one, the one who took music a little more seriously than the others. You always did very well in school without making a big fuss about it. I remember you loved to play with your plastic toy horses. High school with your friends seemed to be a happy time for you. I remember how difficult it was for you to leave them when we moved to another city.

You were active in the local theater. I was really impressed how well you did in several roles. Remember "Wind in the Willows" and "The Seagull?" Then college. You were the last to leave. I recall your excitement, driving over to your college, and your joy in seeing your old high school friend from our previous city.

Then the bombshell! After your freshman year, you quietly let us know you considered yourself to be a lesbian. At first that was hard to take. We accepted what you said, but we did not talk about it. We went through the process which, we have since learned, many loving parents go through in the same situation. We first secretly denied it, thinking, "Oh, this is just a phase. Things will be different later." Then we felt guilty about it, "It must be our fault. What did we do wrong?" We worried about what kind of life you would have, but finally, over a period of years we came to accept your gayness.

Then, eighteen years later, just when your brother came down with leukemia and we were all struggling to deal with that, you dropped the other bombshell. You announced you might be a transsexual. At first I considered your timing was not very good on this one, but later I decided perhaps it was the best of all. While being concerned about your brother, we could not spend as much time worrying about you; and vice versa. It was a difficult time for us, but maybe the worrying time was cut in half while we did double duty!

Your announcement was hard to take, although by then we

had had considerable experience comforting many other PFLAG parents. Working through our feelings and arriving at acceptance probably went a little quicker, but, still, all the stages of grief were there. We just recognized them more quickly.

We could understand your decision also. Your feelings did not match how you were living, and you had just not been aware of, nor considered, the alternatives before. Now there was more information and you understood yourself better then than ever before. Perhaps we should not have been so surprised. Looking back, I now realize there were some subtle hints earlier. In several of the stories you had written as a teenager, the main character was a man, written in first person, sometimes with a sexual theme. The way you preferred to dress was, undeniably, more male-oriented than female. Even in a recording of one of your concerts, when we played it again and finally "listened," you commented that, " I had always wanted to be a boy...." I'm sorry we did not hear you sooner!

So, just as your mother had previously taken the initiative in getting involved with PFLAG, she now jumped with both feet into the transsexual movement. The rest, as they say, "is history." Your mom is very active in promoting the rights of all sexual minorities now, and I support that completely. I tag along to do what I can. She says it is useful that I am there, even if I'm often not sure, myself.

Then we lived through the "step by step" experience of watching and hearing of your progress during the transition. The bouts with the psychiatrist, the beginning of hormones, the school complications, new career, switching public restrooms, name change, changing from F to M on your driver license -- all necessitated by your transition and recognition of your true gender. The break up of your long relationship with your partner was, I know, very difficult, as well as selling a home you loved. But you did it and handled it all very well.

You now seem to me to be happier and more confident in your outlook. You are holding and advancing in a good job. Buying another house was, perhaps, a scary decision, but one which certainly makes economic sense. Now, three years (is it that long?) after your decision to transition, you seem to have a stable, and I hope, happy life. How wonderful!

The point of this letter is that I want to say, "Thank you, Allen. Thank you for insisting on being who you are, and opening our eyes to greater truths than we knew before." I do not believe I can truly realize how great an effort this must have been for you. I respect you for making yourself go up this difficult road. I am impressed that you knew this was the right thing for you to do, and did it. I admire you for facing each difficulty in your chosen (no, not chosen, necessary) path and, with your now well-exercised equanimity, overcoming it and moving on again. Your struggle with your life and the quest to be who you are has been an object lesson in how to live, and how to deal with life, using to the best advantage the cards you are dealt. I am proud you are my son. I just want you to really understand that.

I love you,<br>Dad

## UPDATE

Dear Allen,

I have been rereading my old letters to you and realize it has been seven years since your transition. You continue to amaze me and to confirm that you know yourself very well. I am pleased by your continuing advancement and satisfaction in your work, your new house, new car, new friends, new activities, and new adventuresomeness. And an overseas hiking trip to where? Congratulations on knowing who you are, and thank you again for teaching us much in the process.

Love,<br>Dad

***

Always be a first rate version of yourself, instead of a second-rate version of somebody else.

-- Judy Garland  (Raquel Rice)

# MOM, DAD, WE NEED TO TALK
## Anne Samson*

*I'm a child of the '60s, have MA's in Humanities and History, and am a technical writer. I've been married thirty years (amazing!), with two kids, two dogs, one cat. My hobbies are reading (regional novels, philosophy and religion, cookbooks), cross stitch and quilting, walking, playing with friends (including my husband), gardening, discovering new music. My philosophy is Live and Let Live.*

Ever since I can remember I've felt something was wrong, but it wasn't until about a year ago that I figured out what it was. Our first-born son, Paul, home from his freshman year in college, began for us the painful and rewarding journey of being trans-parents and this is how we reacted.

Our responses to our child were probably predictable, and probably less than praiseworthy. Are you sure (this is not just your overactive imagination)? Is it possible that you're gay (and just don't want to face it or think we'll accept it)? Is it because you haven't had any sexual experience or close male/female relationships ( and are somewhat fearful of getting into them)? And so on. We came up with every alternative explanation we could think of in order not to have to deal with the unthinkable proposition that our intelligent, sensitive, highly talented firstborn son would have to spend the rest of his/her life coping with a condition only those who have it know much about. I certainly didn't. My image of transgendered people came from TV and movie images of transvestites; at the time, I didn't know the difference.

But you liked trucks, we pleaded. You used to play at being Spiderman and Batman. You were always making Star Wars light sabers and Star Trek laser guns. How can this be? Of course it was also true that as a baby, this child sat on the floor and chatted to the pots and pans, begged me for a swimsuit like my pretty flowered one, and argued emphatically with her dad that she was a girl and not a boy. (We decided that at age two she just didn't have it all straight yet, and dropped the subject, assuming eventually she'd figure it out.)

So many almost unnoticed incidents that we dismissed because they didn't make sense at the time began to fall into place: Paul asking me to teach her to sew, the detailed costumes she made for role-playing games and the unisex or female characters she always played; the interest in relationships, both her own and other peoples; the fact that she had friends of both sexes but never dated, the hatred of sharing a room at camp or in the college dorm. I understood now the depression she went through in junior high and why she went to such lengths to wear the most shapeless and drab clothes. As she explained, she always thought she might grow up to be a woman, but in junior high she had to face the fact that wasn't going to happen. The rush of memories was overwhelming. I was torn between "It can't be so" and "Here's another indication that it is."

No one tells you that when a child turns out to be totally other than you assumed, it is very much like a death. Not that parents of trans people are the only ones who experience this grief, but it is peculiar in that there is often no one around who understands the details and can share similar experiences. What I would have given to know just one trans parent in that first year! In our small town, there is still an element of disgrace in being sexually different than the mainstream; people who will talk about their children doing drugs will not mention that their child is gay, if they even know. To whom can you say, "Well, I used the pronoun 'she' for the first time today?"

So many feelings accompany a parent's initial adjustment. There is fear, wondering what this will mean for my child and her future. There is anger and sadness that you didn't know and didn't guess. There is grief at the loss of dreams. The future becomes a blank because none of the ordinary expectations for a son or daughter necessarily apply. For me there is still sadness that we didn't get to share many of the ordinary mother-daughter things that are so much a part of a daughter's growing up. The inevitable question, "Is it something I did?" haunted us.

Transgenderedness challenges the black and white assumptions we all make about our sexuality, a basic fact of our identity. Was I wrong in teaching her how to sew? Could there be a gender-disorder strain in our family tree? There was almost no literature in the local library to answer these questions, and we knew nothing about the Internet, even if we had had access to it.

Fortunately, a few trusted friends and our son-now-daughter, Marie, came to the rescue. Marie provided us with articles she'd received from a trans support group in a nearby large city. She even took me to a meeting where I got to meet, not the flashy transvestites I'd seen on TV, but real, live children, husbands, and wives who talked honestly about the challenges and joys of their daily lives, and who spoke compassionately about us, their friends and family. The information I gained from them helped immeasurably both in my own adaptation and in explaining to friends and family who were as ignorant as I was. The most important fact, and the one least understood, is that being a trans is not a choice; it is a self-discovery.

Adapting to our child's new identity was a challenge for our couple relationship. For a long time we were unable to talk about it with each other in much detail. My reaction was to want to talk endlessly about the revelation, search for information, and speculate on the causes and consequences. My husband's way of dealing with difficult material has always been not to talk much about it until he settles it in his own mind. At some point we each trusted longtime friends with the information, and from there the circle gradually extended, as Marie's initial revelation rippled through family and friends.

The hardest task was telling family, immediate and extended. Endless questions bubbled up. How will this affect our other child? What will the extended family's reaction be? Will they reject me or my child because of this revelation? We asked Marie to tell the family she felt she wanted to tell, as we figured that was both her prerogative and also good practice for a string of future explanations. Our son, younger by two years, took the news without much outward reaction. As a late teenager, he had his own life to live and was pretty immersed in it. Like his father, he processes things slowly, but he nearly always comes out on the

47

side of love and inclusion.

Marie's grandmother was concerned, but accepting. My husband's brother was puzzled. My two sisters were incensed, blaming companions, rebellion, or denial about homosexuality. That Marie was the first child in the extended family, and that they had doted on him/her for years made the revelation hard for them to accept. Also, they didn't see Marie often enough to get used to this new person emerging from her cocoon. To their credit, they have come to accept the fact that Paul is now Marie. They are not comfortable conversing about the subject, but they are all polite and do care about her, despite the fact they think she must be nuts to live as female and to plan to undertake surgery.

In the beginning, my own communication with Marie about the subject was not much more extensive than that of my sisters. Rather than inundate her with the confused storm of feeling I experienced at first, I chose instead to confide in a trusted friend and in my husband. This allowed me to express the fear and anger more freely. I didn't want to say things to Marie I might later regret, and I wanted to move through my selfish concerns to some position from which I could relate to Marie hereafter. What it finally came down to was that, in a choice between my cherished ideas of my child and a relationship with the child herself, I would much rather have the latter. One doesn't quit loving just because the lovee turns out not to be the person you thought he was.

Eventually Marie and I did have the relief of talking together about that initial time. It was a difficult period for both of us, I think. I hadn't realized, nor maybe had she, that we would have to develop a whole new relationship. Nor had I realized that she would have to go through all the stages from early teen to her current age, as she worked to get through the female socialization she missed as a male teenager. Again I was faced with myself. I did not enjoy being a 13-year-old female, myself, and I did not enjoy learning to relate to one. Luckily, we both made it through that phase.

I can now report that it is possible for both children and parents to survive that difficult first few years of trans adjustment. As parents, we may have lost a son, but we have gained a daughter who seems much happier and more a spontaneous than she did before. I like to think that we as parents have gained in tolerance and compassion as we struggled to rethink our assumptions about gender identity and sexuality. Despite our fears for her future and her difficult time searching for a job in our city, Marie has begun a career on the west coast, and is enjoying the freedom she finds there. We talk weekly, exchanging information about books, cooking, decorating, and upcoming events. Probably I'm less tempted than I might have been to offer advice. Having never parented a trans child before, I am not aware of any norms that one should abide by. We pretty much concentrate on the present as it unfolds.

At some point, Marie plans to go for surgery and although I have some fears, I feel that Marie and we will deal with whatever transpires. I have seen her exhibit great courage and determination as she works to make a life for herself. I am very proud to have such an amazing child.

## UPDATE

The latest is that our daughter has been living happily in the Northwest, having had the surgery a couple of years ago. She's fallen in love with the north country and would someday like to buy a place. She does web design for a living, but in her off hours she does search and rescue in the mountains, sharpshoots and hunts, sews, cooks, gardens a little, does photography and leatherwork, writes, keeps a cat, and sees friends. Did I mention that I love her?

# AN EMOTIONAL TRAVELOGUE
## Sherry & Hank Pangborn

*Sherry and Hank have six children and three grandchildren. Hank is a Doctor of Ministry and a retired United Methodist Minister and U.S. Navy Chaplain. Sherry does everything else! Their hobbies are traveling, reading, enjoying the Pacific Northwest lifestyle, but most of all being part of their children's lives. Their children vary greatly in politics, religion, careers and even national origin.*

Travel was always my first love. Whether actually going to a foreign country or simply reading a travel magazine or historical novel, I (Sherry) was captivated. I never thought about "emotional travel" until our last child, my "baby," began hinting that she was going through some gender identity searching, which ultimately ended in her becoming a female-to-male person. This was a trip that I was unprepared to make, and I didn't just rush out and sign up for the journey!

Britt had come out to us as a lesbian at age 16, and my husband and I had become active in both our local PFLAG and also in another group advocating for the GLBT community. We had many happy experiences at local Gay Pride parades and picnics, and watching the Seattle's Men's Chorus (a gay chorus) perform locally in our small county. We knew several transgender people -- but by and large we distanced ourselves from the "t" in "GLBT" out of what I now recognize as uncertainty and a foreboding that our own child was heading in that direction.

And so, as Britt began to leave more books and information around the house about trans issues, we knew we were about to begin another journey. There was never any thought of not supporting her in this venture .. but I think that both my husband and I hoped that the final destination wouldn't really become a reality, and that we could all carry on in the comfort of having gay

50

(not transgendered) children. By this time, a second daughter had come out to us, and was enjoying a relationship with a special woman she had met several months earlier. Our other four children are "straight" but diverse in many other ways.

Because we are now completely accepting of our new son Alex, once known as Britt, I have to stop and remember that the road to this point wasn't an easy one. I always admit to other parents that it was a struggle, and I wondered if I could ever grasp the "t" concept completely. This was a journey I never wanted to make; yet I knew it was one that I had already embarked on and had to complete if we were all to come out whole. Most importantly, I wanted our child to concentrate on her own transition and feelings, and not to have to carry us on her back all the way up the mountain. I knew it was an enormous struggle for her, even without having to take into account our feelings and those of her siblings.

The very first step, trying to remember to call Britt "Alex," was difficult. I resented having to give up the name my husband and I had chosen so carefully for our baby. It held meaning for us, and she had been "Britt" for 21 years. And yet, calling her "Alex" was really such a simple request. I literally agonized over that small request -- and slipped frequently (and still do occasionally) -- which I'm sure was my mind's way of baulking!

Alex started on hormones and seemed very excited by the results. His voice deepened. He could no longer sing like Joan Baez and I was devastated. Music had been a big part of his teen years. He was pleased, but we were wary. I was worried about the effects of testosterone: was it safe? What are the long-term consequences? Some months later, Alex approached me and talked about having "top surgery" (a double mastectomy). I recoiled. Mutilation was how I saw it. In time I decided to offer to pay for the procedure, perhaps hoping to "call his bluff" and see if this was really something Alex wanted desperately. It was, and so we headed for San Francisco for the surgery in January of 2001. It was successful, and it was a turning point for me. Alex was thrilled with the results and seeing his joy seemed to propel me forward in my process. I felt peaceful for the first time in a long time.

Alex is happier than I have seen him in years, and is thriving. He has always been a person with tremendous strength of character and resolve. That in itself helped me through my own process, realizing he would never embark on something like this if it was just a whim or phase. He has always been true to himself, and I admire that. He is emotionally strong, and able to look out for his own happiness and determine the direction of his life.

His fiancée is an amazing girl, a lesbian who has been with him throughout the entire process. She too is strong and has a firm sense of who she is and where she is going in her life. One of our greatest fears was that she might find it overwhelming at some point and not be able to remain in the relationship. Loving her as we do, it would have been terribly painful if that had been the case. They are planning to marry in September of this year, and my husband will officiate at their nuptials! To say we are proud of Alex and Katherine is an understatement.

I have learned a great deal on this emotional journey about what is truly important and what is not. Each person must follow his own destiny and have the strength to empathize but not give in to those who cannot support them and/or try to thwart their progress. By and large, the trans people I have encountered along the way have a seemingly endless supply of courage and dignity.

We give gold medals to our athletes and to our service men and women; yet there are no medals of any sort for the person who confronts his or her own gender confusion and marches forth bravely into the unknown, with or without the support of friends and family. Our trans loved ones have so much heart!

What have I done with the memories of "my little girl" that remain? I think I have put them in an emotional storage unit somewhere in the recesses of my mind. They no longer cause me any pain or wishful thinking. That "little girl" will always be there, with all the precious memories that go along with our life with her. Today we are looking forward, with our son, Alex, to making new memories, traveling new roads, exploring new ideas and gratefully embracing every blessing we have been given. Alex bought us a ticket to the most intriguing and mysteriously rewarding journey of our lives. Thanks, Alex.

# A TRANSSEXUAL IN TEHERAN
## Zari Ghasemi*

*I was born in 1947 in Teheran, Iran into a well-educated middle-class family with four siblings. I married a college classmate. We then went to England to continue our education. While there, I gave birth to our first child, a son, in 1970. We returned to Iran in 1974 and in 1978 our second child, Noosheen, was born. I will be referring to Noosheen as "my daughter" whenever I speak of her, even her childhood, because I have come to believe this individual has really been a girl all along.*

It was in Iran in the early years after the Revolution of 1970 that our daughter, Noosheen, grew up. While we had no idea what to think, we knew from the beginning that her behavior was totally different from our older son's; she liked to play with my dresses, shoes and other clothes. When Noosheen was four I took her to a psychologist. The specialist advised us not to show any reaction to what she did. I began to grow concerned about her effeminacy because, in our environment, differences were not tolerated.

As Noosheen started school we remained concerned about her, but I realize now that we were not really seeing everything; she was learning to hide some of her more unacceptable behavior in reaction to our scolding. Occasionally, however, when I caught her I kept saying to myself that she would grow out of it, without really facing up to what it was. When she was ten I saw a psychiatrist who said Noosheen was effeminate because she identified too closely with me. He advised us to have her spend more time with my husband and his adult male friends. We wanted to do whatever we could to ensure that she would grow up healthy and "normal." We were afraid she might develop into an outcast; her life could even be in danger.

53

Nothing seemed to work. We simply could not change Noosheen's ways. By the time she was about eleven years old, she had grown very withdrawn. She never played with the boys in the neighborhood and, at this age, the neighborhood girls did not like to play with her as much as before. At this age, children were invariably separated by gender. It was actually considered to be a violation of norms and social standards for a "boy" to be around girls much at this age. We were concerned about Noosheen's present and future. Stigma was attached to us and to her for being different. Even our immediate family was making derogatory remarks. (In retrospect, everyone was avoiding saying the most obvious fact, which was that even at this young age Noosheen was showing signs that she was homosexual, the only thing anybody could think of.)

In Iran, families are very close and their judgment is very important. The community in general is closed and very judgmental.

By her teenage years, Noosheen was more and more withdrawn. I realize now that she was terrified to tell us what was happening to her. It is hard for my husband and me to deny that we, too, were affected by the sharply intolerant society we lived in, even becoming reluctant to take Noosheen out with us. Only seven years ago did Noosheen finally confide in me the extent to which she had been brutally mistreated. She told me how she had been constantly ridiculed, assaulted, pushed down and beaten in the stomach by her classmates while others just watched.

Now even finding the right school for Noosheen was a problem because they screened students, not only on the basis of academic merit, but also on their beliefs, conformity to the set standards in terms of clothing, behavior, etc. Noosheen was not an irresponsible or disruptive student by any standard, but she did not conform to the mainstream of that society and that put her at a great disadvantage. We started getting warnings that she should not mix with students older than herself. (All schools in Iran are single sex only; this meant Noosheen had to attend an all boys' school).

Noosheen had an excellent academic record, and we were prepared to pay higher tuition to get her into a better, stricter school, which we hoped would "cure" her problems. We succeeded in finding a relatively good school that could guarantee to some extent that Noosheen had a place in a university in Iran. This was very important because achieving entry into an Iranian university is not easy.

While attending this new school, Noosheen's situation deteriorated. The school was extremely intolerant of her non-conformity. Noosheen started experiencing depression, becoming withdrawn and fearful. She was also in love with one of her male classmates. Again it was only much later that she told me about how much pressure she had experienced during this time, how her classmates still ridiculed her, as a non-conforming "boy."

It was the last year of high school when Noosheen became extremely depressed and unhappy. This time we took her to a doctor, a specialist in teenage sexual problems, who diagnosed Noosheen as a transsexual after six months. At this time Noosheen would not talk to my husband or me or any of her friends. She would draw the curtains in her room, remain isolated and cry hysterically. Even then we thought of it as homosexuality, the only condition we understood. Noosheen was even arrested twice by the police because of the same thing -- that her behavior was that of a homosexual. Transsexuality was hardly known in that society. (I have heard they now talk about it in the media and there have been a couple of books on the subject in the last few years in Iran.)

In the meantime, Noosheen attempted suicide as a way out. During a six-month period she attempted suicide ten times. She cut herself. She used sleeping tablets, and once she tried all the medicine in the medicine cabinet. As we realized that Noosheen was desperately trying to find a way out of her unbearable life, we became more sympathetic and supportive although we were devastated.

By the summer before Noosheen's last year of high school, I had been working in a very demanding job. As Noosheen was going through these intense difficulties, and needed a great deal of attention I decided to seek leave from work. Because I could not explain any part of the reason for this I eventually lost a very rare, good job. But I could not risk Noosheen's life to stay at work.

Meanwhile Noosheen was extremely fearful of leaving the

house and refused to go to school; even private evening classes did not work out. We knew by this time that the only way to survive was to find a way to take her out of the country. Any time she went out she could be arrested. Her future safety as well as her possibilities of advancing in Iranian society (education, employment) seemed very bleak.

My husband managed to get Noosheen exempted from the military service. Then, after a long struggle with the British Embassy in Tehran, we took her to England, but her presence there made our older son very uncomfortable. I decided then to leave for the United States. I came to the USA in October 1996 and in June 1997 Noosheen entered the USA to join me. My husband had flown with her to the U.S. Embassy in Vienna to obtain a special visa, as my minor child. My husband still works in Iran, however, and can spend only a couple months a year here.

## UPDATE

After completing a master's degree I have been working as a public school teacher for two years and am working on a visa. My daughter graduated from a university in New York last year and has been working for a year.

In view of the above my fear of running into financial difficulties that could jeopardize Noosheen's future and her surgery has subsided to some extent. Noosheen has been transitioning; that is, she's been on hormones for four years, she's had a tracheal shave, she's almost through with the electrolysis , and she's been living full time as a female for more than three years.

Emotionally she's much better in terms of self-esteem and confidence. She is in a relationship with a man who loves her very much. Noosheen has put down her name for the SRS and she's supposed to have it in 2004. As for myself, I am happy that I was able to be with my daughter during her first years of transition, which looked to me like a birth of a new child.

# PART III

# INVENTIVE LOVE RELATIONSHIPS

# Shock and Confusion -- With Love
## Madeline Rivers*

*For a very private person, this is difficult for me to share. But the lack of stories and information about transgendered partners pushes me to share my own thoughts so that others might learn.*

My spouse of 12 years informed me a few months ago of his transgenderedness. I became scared and confused. Yet, celebrating his future goal of happiness, i.e., becoming his true self, eventually became easy for me to accept. It just seemed natural. Many strange things that I look back upon, I can now understand. I just thought that he was gay. Well, my own woman's intuition needs a 30-year check up because I was only half right. I see that most of our lives together has enabled us to get him/her to this point. Brent/Betty is in the safest city, at a job with the most accommodating company policies, and available support groups. Thank goodness for his high intellect that lets him think things through. If I had been approached at the beginning of our relationship, I doubt I'd had written this article.

Information, information, information. I need pamphlets, anything to see what others have felt and done. What happens to the spouse of a M2F?

I've been shoved into the rarest of rare categories. Why? Because most partners leave before the shock wears off. Did I think about it? Of course I did, I'm human; but I'm also in love with a rare and wonderful person. Brent/Betty is still the same person I've loved all these years; he/she just wants to do it in heels!

What a mind bender! He says he loves me and his attraction is the same. So, boy/girl loves and is attracted to girl. Girl still loves boy/girl but is naturally attracted to boys. I love Brent/ Betty but the attraction is not natural to me. Our love for each other is the same. While he/she is dealing with gender issues, it forces me to deal with my sexuality issues. I feel like I'm in a dramatic soap opera. Living like this certainly isn't boring.

We have always had "bedroom issues;" at least now I know why. I understand that Brent/Betty is driven to the changes she is making. However, I am still driven to be with males. By acknowledging the "big pink elephant" in our marriage, in one night my big strong, sensitive husband became a woman who is also a lesbian. This also cut me off from my natural adult drives.

But here is the hardest part of the relationship for me. All the things that I found attractive about Bill, like his size, hands, and strength are exactly the things that he despises about himself. Talk about a turnoff!

Brent/Betty is just starting to transition. By the time this publication is out, she will be living full-time as a woman. At one point I was so confused and unsure of my own femaleness that I thought I'd hunt down the first male I could find. I know it's natural. So, I went to Brent/Betty before I destroyed our delicate relationship with infidelity.

He asked me to love just the "person I've loved all these years." It was odd; she loved me with a talent and skill normally considered between female lovers. The imagined gestures that would have made me feel uncomfortable or strange never came. Yes, it was certainly one-sided and all for me. I think she was happy to be able to show her love for me when words weren't enough.

It's getting harder in every phase of our life. I'm trying to support her through this difficult transition. We are both seeing our own therapists and he has multiple support groups that I thank God for daily. I am working on a "Genetic Ladies Auxiliary" group for my own support. There are three ladies still with their M2F partners that are going to join. I believe where there is one, there are others that need the support and love. I'm keeping my fingers polished with his favorite basecoat, hoping for the best.

- - - -

Note: I smile as I read through this and notice my inconsistent use of pronouns, but my editor won't let me change it. She says I was very brave to write this in the midst of my own confusion. I realize now that changing pronouns is one of the most difficult things about loving a transgendered person. Maybe other spouses will understand and know they are not alone.

# SILENCE = DEATH
## Tamara Alexander
### (for Max)

*I have been wedded in spirit to Max Beck, member of the Intersex Society of North America, for almost five years. We live in Atlanta, Georgia, with our three cats. When I am not writing papers I am busy raising our three cats, and the consciousness of Emory psychology undergraduates.*

We met in college, the first day of spring semester, junior year. Having had an earlier class in that room, I stayed on. She was the first to arrive. Our eyes met across an empty classroom; the neon signboard in my head lit up; something was forever changed. I would spend the next two years chasing down the mystery behind that moment.

We became friends. Dinners at each other's houses. Study groups. Movie marathons. We even had a date -- candlelight and wine, out alone, glowing at each other across the table. And I told myself that I had been wrong, that she was straight. Hell, she even got married. I resolved to live with that.

It wasn't until April of the following year that I finally told her about the one and only love affair I'd ever had with a woman, and she responded in kind. I thought that this bit of history must have been what I'd been reading when we first met -- not that she didn't have feelings for women, just that they had not been about me. How could I have known how wrong I would be?

I returned home to Georgia after graduation. I held her hand In the procession and reminded myself that this was where it ended. She was happily married, and I was adrift. We started a correspondence, ostensibly because she had missed out on having someone to talk to when she was figuring out her sexual orientation, and wanted to be that person for me. She was finally talking to me, after two years, about being a lesbian.

We were peeling the onion, one layer at a time. In my

confusion, I reunited with my ex. It was only then that she wrote to tell me how involved she really had been, how deeply it hurt her to have missed our chance, how badly she really had wanted to be with me. I wrote back that I loved her. That I expected to live with the ache of that regret for the rest of my life.... I sent her Robert Frost's "The Road Not Taken," copying it out by hand on the back of the envelope, sitting on the floor of a bookstore. She left Harold.

We spoke at all hours of the day over the next two weeks. I called her at work. "I need to come see you." I had expected her excitement, joy, anticipation. She sighed. Her tone was ominous. "Okay," she said. "Come. We'll talk. There are some things you should know about me." "That sounds serious," I said. She agreed, "It is." My first thought was that she had cancer. My next thought was much closer to the mark.

The visit was to be two weeks later. The topic kept coming back; there were things that I should know about her. She didn't want to talk about them over the phone. Panic would break into her voice at the subject. "Why are you so afraid to tell me?" I asked. "Nothing could change the way I feel about you." "This could, " she said. "It's horrid." Eventually the strain of not talking about it won out, and she told me. By this time, I was already fairly certain what she was going to say.

"When I was born, the doctors couldn't tell whether I was a boy or a girl." She dictated the speech as if she'd told it many times before and all of the emotion had fallen right out of it. I finally heard the complete story of her college affair with a woman, who had said six words in bed that altered the entire course of Max's life: "Boy, Judy, you sure are weird." Max told me she knew then that she was a lesbian, but one who could not be with women because they would know how her body was different. She married Harold because men were just less sensitive to the subtleties of women's anatomy.

My response was tears, "I can't believe you've been carrying this around by yourself your whole life." I hadn't been surprised; growing up in a house full of medical texts had acquainted me with intersexuality. I was not, as she had feared, horrified, repulsed, or anxious.

"What did you think," she asked me in the car as I was preparing to write this essay about loving her, "what did you expect my body to be like? "I thought it would be mysterious and wonderful," I told her. "And it was."

I went up to Philadelphia for four short days over her birthday in February. We attempted to cook, burned the butter, and collapsed in each others' arms on the floor. We left the house only to pick up take-out and Ben & Jerry's Wavy Gravy ice cream. Nonetheless, for the first two nights, she would not take off her boxer shorts. I could feel the wonder of her pressing against me through the flannel, but I was not allowed to touch. Although the rest of her body lay out before me to be charted, the triangle of flesh between her legs was a guarded region. She told me she couldn't lubricate because of the scar tissue, and because the surgeons had taken her labia to make a vaginal opening when she was fifteen. "Lots of women can't lubricate," I told her. "That's why they make feminine lubricants."

We decided to go shopping. In the feminine hygiene aisle, we compared the relative merits of Gyne-Moistrin and its competitors. When I looked up at Max, her eyes were wide and glazed. She was shaking. Her breath was irregular. I picked up the nearest product, sent her outside to wait, and paid at the register. We went home.

That night we slept downstairs in front of the fire. It was February 5, her 29th birthday. There was easily a foot of snow on the ground and it had all frozen over. Only her boxers still remained between us. Later that night she went upstairs to the bathroom, and when she slipped back under the covers, my hands slid from one end of her body to the another. The boxers were gone. I will never be able to recapture the magic of that moment. "Ohhh!" She was terrified, and I was aware of her fear and the cost of offering herself up to me in that moment. I have never wanted to pleasure someone, never wanted to offer my hands and my fingers to heal and to love and to delight, I have never been so awed by the feeling of touching as I was that night. I wanted to stroke and explore and learn and know every inch of her, the lines and crevasses from scars and healings, the tight cavern which held my fingers so tightly. She pulled me down on top of her and wrapped her arms around me and came, calling my name, sobbing against my shoulder. And I wept with her.

I wept for the loss of what she hadn't had and the lovers who hadn't reveled in the wonder of her body, wept for what I hadn't had before I held her in love, and I am weeping as I write this now.

It was a full year before she let me touch her that way again. A full year. We were still taking baby steps toward completely open lovemaking. Still peeling onions.

We moved to Atlanta in the summer of 1995. Broken by the stresses of new jobs, financial worries, lack of friends and supports, and a 1904 bungalow which we loved but could barely afford renovating, Max lapsed into a depression. She began to tell me that she was a monster and she just shouldn't be here. The day she did not go to work because she was planning to hang herself, I took her to the hospital. It was the hardest thing I have ever done in my life.

I had the unenviable task of surrendering the illusion that my unconditional love and acceptance were going to save her. No matter how much I loved her, no matter what I would give to heal her, I was not enough. I could not keep her safe. I could not erase thirty years of grief and doubt about her worth and her place in this world.

I was isolated from other people in ways I hadn't been before; no one knew her past medical history, and she was not ready for me to talk to anyone else about it. My friends from Philly called to check on me; they loved me and understood only that I was in agony because Max was depressed. They assured me that she would get better, that she would come home to me and the beautiful life we had created together. I was not certain she could ever recover from the damage that had been done.

I read her medical records over and over. Sorted through John Money's articles left from college psych classes. Read her journal, trying to understand. At night, I screamed my lungs out at the sheer futility of trying to help her. I had nightmares of surgeons wielding shiny scalpels, tying her down, and rearranging her body. I wept at work. I wept at home. I did endless battle with our mounting financial doom; the mortgage was late, the car unpaid, utilities coming due -- all without her income. How would I ever keep things intact so that she had a life to return

I read her records, and I wondered, if this had happened to me, if my body had been desecrated and abused and held up in public life for the amusement of interns, would I have survived it even half as well as she had? Would I have had the courage to go on for thirty years with the memory of those rapes, my mother's shame and my own, and the lies of doctors?

I made promises to keep myself sane. I swore that I would not lose her. I swore that I would not allow this to happen to anyone else. I promised myself that if she slid off the face of this earth out of the exhaustion of fighting for her right to exist, I would not allow this to happen to any child like her. I would find out how and by whom this awful process was being perpetuated, and I would make it stop.

It took four months. Three hospitalizations. Persistent suicidal ideation and unwavering depression. She lost her job because she couldn't stop crying. I dragged her to monthly support group meetings in the gender community. I made her return calls to Cheryl Chase at ISNA. I pushed her to call the people Cheryl sent out to make contact with her. Each time, she would feel a little less alone, and a little more hopeful. And then the depression would creep back, telling her to give up. Telling her she would never be whole, would never be accepted, would never be anything but a shameful secret. As many times as I had learned in that first precious year together that love is an amazing healer, I had still to learn that sometimes shame and blatant evil can be stronger.

It is now almost a year since that last depression. It still creeps up on us from time to time. When she doesn't come home on time, I have to pace myself not to panic. I have to remind myself that not being home does not mean she has killed herself. But the danger is always there. It's only in the last few weeks that it feels less close, less powerful than myself. Less powerful than the sense of self I'm amazed and awed to watch her discover.

She has cut her hair, embraced butch, and found a good endocrinologist. We marched together in the parade at Gay Pride. I have come to believe myself a part of this community. I may not be transgendered, transsexual, or intersexed. I may have been fortunate enough to be born into a body that matches my sense of self and is accepted by society in its original form. But this is still my fight.

There is a popular slogan in the gay community that proclaims "silence = death." Her silence, and mine, almost meant her death. I am reminded of the words of the clergyman who recalled that during the Holocaust he did not speak because he was not a member of any of the groups being rounded up for execution. When they came for him, there was no one left to speak for him.

She is my partner, my love, the greatest gift life ever gave me. I choose to honor her decision to stay alive. I choose to speak on a daily basis. I honor her courage and her complexity. If she walks between the worlds set up by a gender-dichotomous society, then that is where my path leads as well.

## UPDATE

Max has since recovered from his depression, and in 1998 chose to transition to a male gender role. We were married at home in 2000, and welcomed our daughter Alder Elizabeth into the world that May. We continue to build a life together. Partners of intersexuals are welcome to contact me through the editor for mutual support.

I'm beginning to believe that LIFE is transition... we're constantly changing and evolving... grasping new ideas and concepts... opening our horizons to new people, new ways of "living"... life IS transition. Laura Hugh (Cindy Scott)

# RELATIONSHIP TOOLS
## Samantha Star Straf

*I am a thirty-something computer programmer living in Lawrence, Kansas where my partner is working on a Ph.D. Some of the ways that I describe myself are: geek, bisexual, polyamorous, Unitarian-Universalist, pagan, science fiction and fantasy fan, friend, owned by a cat, sheltie owner, and folk music fan.*

My partner, Pooch, and I had been close friends for almost ten years before we started dating. He had come to terms with his crossdressing and had decided that next time he got involved with someone he would tell them up front, so on our second date I was handed a stack of photos and told, "I want to share something special about myself with you." My first reaction was to wonder who his girlfriend was, then I realized the similarity and with a sigh of relief said, "This is you." I was the first person outside the transgender community to ever know about Andrea. I think the fact that this was phrased in a positive manner and that I found out early on in the relationship made my journey easier than for most partners.

My first concern was the fact that Andrea (my partner's alter-ego) was in the closet. I had gone through the coming out process of my bisexuality many years before, and realized that it is very hard for me to live with a secret, so the first compromise we made was that she would have to come out more. I wanted permission to tell my friends and not have to watch what I say. Together we have brought Andrea out of the closet slowly (leaving much more room for her clothes <grin>), starting with telling Pooch's best friends. Luckily almost all the reactions have been loving and positive. Some family members either do not know or do not want to talk about it, but almost everyone else knows. This puts me at ease since I don't have to remember who does or does not know a secret. It also keeps me from having to watch what pronoun I use since I tend to switch back and forth. Since then, we have both done a variety of community education talks and outreach.

The next issue we struggled with was time. For a while Pooch was so excited at having an accepting partner that there was much more Andrea time than Pooch time. Considering that for the first two years we lived half a continent apart, this made for some struggles. We decided to make sure there was equal time scheduled in each gender. For every Andrea visit there was also a Pooch visit. One trick I learned from a significant others list was to have Pink/Blue days. I have the right when I put an event on the calendar to mark it either Pink (I want Andrea at this event) or Blue (I want Pooch at this event). If it doesn't have a color then it doesn't matter to me which presentation is there.

One of Andrea's time issues is the time it takes her to get ready. I am not one to fuss with makeup and hair and it bothered me to have to wait for her. We both compromised on this one. With more practice and electrolysis the time to get ready has cut down and I have learned to have a book to read and remind her in plenty of time to start getting ready. One specific learning compromise on this happened when we went to a science fiction convention together; there was a morning panel that I wanted to attend and I also wanted to get breakfast. She was having a bad hair day and would just not be ready in time to make both. Our financial agreement for that weekend was that I was paying for the food. To make things balance, I offered to go get some carryout breakfast but she would have to pay for it and to promise to be ready in time for the panel. We both got what we needed. We have learned to be specific on needs versus wants, to let the other know what is important, and be open to creative solutions.

When I first found out about Andrea, I read all the books I could find about transgenderism, got on many e-mail lists, and submerged myself in information. One of the fears that I found was that many transsexuals start as crossdressers and later decide that they want to transition. I did not think I could handle that. Even though Pooch said he was a crossdresser I still had fears. I decided that a "I will promise to be your friend but I can-not promise to be your partner if you decide to transition" statement would make me feel much more comfortable. Over time he has changed his gender identification to crossdresser-plus and now as transgendered. He still has no plans to transition full time but neither of us has ruled that out as a possibility.

Pooch has been very good about checking with me about any steps that might be intimidating for me. Before he started electrolysis he dug out all the old photos of him with beard and we talked about what I would miss if he got electrolysis. When he was looking into hair loss options, we compromised on a topical application until there was more research because I feared any negative side effects. When he decided he wanted some breast growth we took a year to discuss the options, to make sure this was what he wanted and that we were aware of potential consequences. I was against surgical augmentation and also nervous about hormones. We decided to have a year-long test period where he wore breast forms every day, even when in boy mode, to be certain this is what he wanted, and to give me time to get used to the idea. After that year he started on hormones with a planned three months off after a year. Together we reevaluated after the three-month "off" period. Today my partner is back on hormones and happy with their effects. I'm still concerned with some of the side effects, but am beginning to believe that this won't "escalate" to full transition, or if it does, that it will be over a long period of time and will be a journey we take together.

...and then the day came when to remain tight in a bud was more painful than the risk it took to blossom.
—Anais Nin  (Niece of Alexis)

# STILL HETERO?
## Erica Musselman

*My partner is an FTM named Bren.*
*We were best of friends for eight years and*
*then, two years ago, we got together. She*
*(soon to be he) is, also, still my best friend.*

I decided when we started our new journey together to keep it hidden from my family. They are very old-fashioned; they believe that anything or anyone who is not straight is wrong and disgusting. Somehow I was able to detach myself from this horrible way of thinking and became a more open-minded and liberal person.

At age 23 I decided to make the change in my life style. Before Bren and I got together, I was your "normal straight hetero female." We had been very close throughout our friendship. I waited about three months, but then I could not lie to my mother any longer. I was hoping that because I was her daughter that she would still love me and accept me for who I was and what I decided to do. I was wrong; she did just the opposite. I have not been able to talk to my mother or family for over a year. The only family member that I can have a relationship with is my sister, who has been very supportive.

Bren has asked me on many occasions (not so much any more) if I regret the decision I made to be with a transgender. I always reply with the same answer, "I love you and our life together and I would never change a thing." I have struggled with the fact I do not have a family any longer, but I am 25 years old now and it is time to be a grownup. I feel very lucky to have all that I do have in my life. I am very glad this happened when it did, because I was able to get out of my parent's home and live on my own. I would not have been able to do that if I had been any younger.

Bren's parents have been very supportive during her gender transition and love her no matter what she decides. I wish there could be more parents out there like that. I never used to understand what gay, lesbian and trans went through, just to tell their parents about their "secret." Now I do.

I will say that changing from a traditional "hetero" person to one living with a "trans" partner has improved me greatly. I can only say positive things about my life now. I thought I belonged in the usual "hetero" relationships, but I feel now that I was wrong. I never really enjoyed sex with a "hetero" male. I have never had a more enjoyable sex life than the one with Bren. He and I always say I get the best of both worlds. A bit of male personality and a bit of the female personality come through. I have become more understanding about life around me and to people in other nontraditional situations.

Bren and I have a very open and honest relationship; we always have. In the beginning I had some mixed feelings about the transition; would I wait and stick around until all the surgeries were complete, and would I still love her when "she" becomes a "he"? There is no question in my mind; I am in this for the duration. I have learned to love life and live each day to the fullest. Like I stated earlier, life has only gotten better since we both "came out." In fact, we are very excited about our upcoming commitment ceremony!

So what is my sexual orientation? Even though I am now "marrying" a female, as I think back over my life, I realize I've always preferred men. Perhaps it is, at least partly, the male within Bren that I see and love. Though I questioned it for a while, I think now that I am still a hetero female.

My husband wrote a coming-out letter to his mom. They called the other night. Apparently they are very supportive of us. It almost sounded like they can handle this better than if we had told them we were divorcing...          --The Carltons

# EMERGENCE
## Maureen Kelly

*I am happily heading into the eighth year of life, love and adventure with my partner; together with 27 tropical fish in Ithaca, New York. We live proudly in the middle ground of both sexual orientation and gender identity.*

It all started over antipasto and zucchini parmesan. The quiet corner table in what would become our first apartment together invited the exchange -- something about that night set it apart, upped the ante. Innocently enough (my companion) put out the question for us to devour more eagerly than the meal that sat before us. "So, what is it about me and bi women?" It hung there -- who would bite first? I was excited and anxious -- god forbid I say the wrong thing or even the truth; either could hurt a lot.

"Well, you like to move as much as I do..." I had defined and evaluated myself so much I had it down to a short and clear understanding -- I like to move, take it all in, I'm not too particular about parts. "What?" What now? How do you back=pedal from that one? What could I really say? How about, well, simply enough, Honey, I think you take being a big ole butch dyke to another level, you do more, you experience life from more than one place, but not really two, you've kind of created your own space and it works. You don't just pull it off, you do it with grace and style, and I love that.

I suddenly had this amusing vision of a blue and red polka-dot Little Red Riding Hood doll I had when I was a kid. It was the kind of doll you could turn upside-down, flip the dress over and voila -- a new doll emerged. But it was more than your average two-dimensional plaything -- you could find Little Red, Grandma and the Wolf with the proper pulling, flipping and shifting. I kept this revelation to myself for the time being.

"So, you know how I look out at people and there aren't any gender filters -- well, I think you look at yourself and there aren't any, either..." A wave crossed the table, not a devastating tidal wave but a clarifying one, one that clears away all the rubble so you have an unencumbered view of the shining shell lying below. A short, thoughtful smile surfaced, "yeh."

We've had a knack for creating pictures from the beginning. We're both visual people and sometimes the drawing of a picture gives more clarity when we haven't discovered the words yet. Napkins are a favorite medium -- it seems that the nourishment of a shared meal feeds our brains too. The indented floral background of our tissue-thin napkins help us reveal the unnamed layers we begin to uncover. These pictures have no limits; we draw people and places and sex. We share our past and build our future on paper napkins at home, in restaurants, on road trips, any scrap will suffice; you'd be surprised at what you can fit onto a small paper square. We even branched out to paper placemats one desperate evening in Washington, DC. We'd been traveling and talking all day, tired but still wanting to say more; the pictures emerged over soup and bread.

This particular night we start with me. The drawing: a woman looking out toward the sea of possibilities, the desires and potential attractions not limited by the simple distinctions of physical genders. The next napkin further reveals the truth, I watch the drawing emerge; the image is the reverse of mine. The sea of possibility not bound by physical genders exists on the inside, not out. It got still. Neither of us wanted to move or speak. What's the protocol? There must be some ritual to signify a beginning, a rebirth, the revelation that sat before us needed a marker.

On the phone with an ex-lover we sought out more of the truth. Funny how we look back to make sense of what's ahead. Shared history sometimes helps make sense of reality. What about that record-breaking batting average of ex-girlfriends marrying men? "What do you think..." No shocking revelations, but a previously hidden truth was nudging its way onto the table. "It's not like it was that big of a leap, you know what I mean?" After trying so hard to convince everyone it was just coincidence, perhaps it wasn't after all. Perhaps the mobility of gender expression was expressly what attracted them? It was for me. Imagine: A partner whose identity is as mobile, as fluid as my attraction. The limitless possibilities tingle.

It was sad packing up that corner table and leaving that space behind. A couple of places later we've created new sacred spaces, new revelations that bring us further along. We started keeping the napkins, maybe we'll put together our gender journey coffee-table book someday. Pictures always help. So does the Little Red Riding Hood doll my parents finally sent us a couple summers ago.

## The Waking World - Eight years later

I've always loved that time between awake and asleep. The sun comes through the blinds enough to wake me but let my lover sleep. This is the time when I can move quietly closer -- guards are down. My hand reaches out to caress hair, face, arms. My lover is at peace and safe here with me. No one is looking on with that familiar confusing stare. No one stumbles on pronouns. No one can touch my lover but me.

I have been growing a thicker skin when it comes to the waking world. It can be a hard place for us to be. Sometimes they can't see the love because of their fear. They don't realize the fit, the click, the comfort of my world. I have it all -- the fluidity of my outward expression of love is in perfect synch with my lover's inward expression of self. You see, I have always felt at home in the middle, on a scale of 0 - 6, a true Kinsey 3. I look at people first, gender later; my connections are more profound than parts.

And I've struck gold with my lover. You see, my lover's more at home moving among and around genders; my lover's identity is not bound by physicality. We traverse the richness of our love with a tidal rhythm. The ebb and flow is smooth and natural allowing for outward and inward expressions to compliment and mesh with one another. We braid ourselves together with all our strands.

That is what I know of my love and what makes the hurt hit harder out there in the waking world. Why must they stare? My love isn't good enough? Pure enough? Or is it too much to think of all the options...too much to think there might be more than their scripts? Options can be frightening -- there's a certain simplicity and comfort in multiple-choice questions as long as they end up with one answer. People do like possibilities, but just not too many.

In the waking world love is seen through male/female, straight/gay filters. Filters that have been put in place because of fear and shame and a nervous giddiness born from the wonder of what might happen if we relied less on boxes, labels and rules and more on love and passion.

I'm working on the waking world. I'm loving more and fearing less -- showing myself, my love, and the rest who may watch, that the strength and beauty of my love is far greater than our greatest fears and biggest confusions. Of course there's struggle, but right here, right now, I silently stretch across a sun-stained bed offering my touch, my protection and my love toward our efforts to weather the waking world. I slip back into sleep dreaming of a place with more doors and windows in the walls that surround me.

Incarnated

Swadiksha

Incarnated once more
Pushed outward from the Divine sea
onto the shores of Maya
Welcomed into the arms of earthly mother and father
second son of three
Reflections in the mirror reveal a cruel fate
locked in a gender that's not really me
The adversary delights in the delusion
The surgeon can offer only his blade
Rescued by the Divine teacher
who takes all genders away

# JUST LIKES TO DRESS
## Julie Freeman

*I am the significant other of a cross-dresser. We have been married over 38 years and have two grown daughters. I teach computer software, love books, and enjoy puzzles. I also write articles on crossdressing from a significant other's point of view for our local support group.*

I have known about my husband's crossdressing since 1987. At that time one daughter was in college, the other in high school. When my husband first told me about his crossdressing, my reaction was, "Are you gay?" (And I never knew!!). He said "No, I just like to dress like a woman." My second question was, "Do you want to be a woman?" Again, he said, "No, I just want to dress like a woman." So began many conversations between us. I was, as most SigO's are, bewildered, puzzled, embarrassed, and most of all terrified as I did not know what this meant. I did not know if my husband was out of control. I couldn't sleep, and I got sick! I told him I could not go on this way, and he promised that he would do nothing without my permission. That helped me regain a semblance of my life, and I was able to sleep without worrying that he was going to go out gallivanting when I was asleep.

With little to go on at that time, I remembered that I had seen a show on crossdressing on television. The show was done very well, and I remembered that I had learned there was no cure for crossdressing. I wrote to the show for a tape so as to obtain information on Tri-Ess, a national organization for crossdressers and their families, which had been featured on that talk show.

In time, the tape came; we wrote to Tri-Ess and found out that there would be a convention in our area. I encouraged my husband to go since I believed that he needed to meet other crossdressers and find out what all this meant. He was a bit reluctant to go until I also agreed to attend for a couple of days.

We went to the conference and he was in seventh heaven,

76

of course, meeting other crossdressers for the first time. I had a great time as well which surprised me as I had no idea what to expect. But I met the greatest group of men ever -- sensitive, caring, interested in what I had to say, and intelligent.

When we came home, we were both in tears as we realized that these friends we had made were now flying back home, perhaps even out of our lives. But we did find out about a local group. That scared both of us as we weren't sure we were really ready for anything close by.

But after a few months, we got up the courage to contact the local group, and eventually went to some meetings. In time, we told both our daughters. Their main concern was for me and how I was handling the situation. Since they have now both graduated from college and are no longer living at home, they are not involved in that part of our lives, but they have seen pictures and they know we are active.

Over the next few years, we became very involved with support groups. My husband went on to become founder of a support group in our area, and I became an activist for significant others. I began writing articles from a significant other's point of view and these have been published in many newsletters, on the Internet, and in gender magazines such as The Femme Mirror and Tapestry.

In the last couple of years I have cut back my involvement with the community, but we are both part of a couples group, and I participate in an on-line support group for significant others. I continue to write monthly articles for my husband's support group, and I have a hot-line number listed for other wives/partners new to the phenomenon. My goal is to help other couples put crossdressing into their relationships in a positive manner.

Personally, I have found that my relationship with my husband has deepened significantly since he told me about the crossdressing. He has always been a very kind, considerate, and generous person, and I think there is a direct correlation between these personality traits and his desire to crossdress.

This is not say that I like everything about the cross-dressing. There are times when I feel it impacts too much on our lives, but my husband, being considerate, will back off a bit when I complain. We have learned to compromise. We have learned what each other's boundaries are. Early on, my husband realized that he did not want to bring his "femme" side into the bedroom, so I have not had to face the same sorts of sexual issues that other wives face. I have no problem with what my husband wears to bed -- he could wear a gorilla suit if he wants. That would not turn him into a gorilla!! But I don't care to kiss lipstick and he respects that. So when he is crossdressed, he is my friend, not my lover.

Like most significant others, this is not something I wished for, nor is it something I really like. But I have come to learn that crossdressing is not a choice. I believe it is a biological condition that impacts more men in our society than most of us know. And it is this biological condition which has made my husband the wonderful person I believe he is.

And so we continue day by day working on our relationship. We have our ups and downs, but have learned that that is normal in any relationship, not just marital relationships or, especially, relationships between crossdressers and their spouses.

First they laugh at you,
Then they fight you,
Then you win.
      Mahatma Gandhi
      (Teach Tolerance)

# PART IV

# CRUCIAL OTHERS

# A FAMILY'S JOURNEY

Tarynn M., Sophia, Kim Marie,  Willow Marie,
Misty Layne, and Amber Leigh -- all  Wittens

*It seemed important that we tell our
story as a family.  I am proud that they all
agreed and were as upfront and honest as
they were.  We all hope  our story helps
others. I am a postoperative male-to-female
transsexual research scientist.*

The journey has not been easy for any of us. Our family,
already separated because of my moving to take a new job in a new
state over 1,000 miles away, and then split again due to divorce,
was further stressed by my announcing that I was going to live the
rest of my life as a woman.

### Sophia's Story (mother, age 82)

For some years now, Leon and I had wondered if our son
Matthew was a latent homosexual because of some of his emotional
responses, so that when he informed us that he was seriously
considering making a gender change, we were not entirely in
shock. We suggested he pursue this further with a therapist
knowledgeable in this field of transgendering, but to no avail. I
realized that he would not be swayed and simply accepted it. It
wasn't easy. What would we tell our friends and family -- what
would their reaction be? Above all, how would this affect his
career, his life, his children?

This last was the sore point where Leon (his father) was
concerned. He felt Matthew should wait until the girls were all out
of college and self-sufficient. He worried that we might have to
deplete our retirement resources supporting Matthew and his
family.  His death, at 79, four years ago, released him from all of
his concerns.

Matthew is now legally named Tarynn. I can only be
inspired with the way she has restructured her life and with her
various scholastic achievements. It was my privilege to be able to
attend meetings of persons who were already transgendered or

were planning to be. Listening to their stories was very educational. It made me aware that making this kind of a change was, in many instances, an urgent need and that time, as the person aged, was the enemy. The expense was also a serious obstacle. It was also very sad to hear of the cruel rejections suffered at the hands of close-minded parents. I am happy to say that Tarynn and I are great friends.

### Kim's Story (ex-wife, age 47)

When Matthew told me he was exploring a possible gender change, I was at first shocked, but later things began to make sense. Little clues I had definitely noticed but had easily dismissed came up to the surface. Matthew tried to put me at ease by saying it was just an exploration, but as the weeks and months went by, I got the definite feeling that "Matthew" would soon be a name of the past. In hindsight, I can see that I went through the stages of grief. The consequences of this information getting out seemed enormous to me, so I talked to no one about it for a very long time.

When the kids were told, they did not want anyone to know for fear of being ostracized by their peers. I, personally, believed that we come to this life as a male or a female to experience life from that particular perspective and that there are no accidents. However, recent events in my own life have allowed me to respect Tarynn's decision on a whole new level. Sometimes, in life, we have to make decisions that are terribly difficult. I believe we choose each experience in order to grow as a soul, so how can we not honor this process in others and in ourselves?

Families, of course, are affected by one another and they are all here to experience life and make their own choices in order to grow. I believe we will all be better human beings as a result, although the process is often long, difficult and sometimes overwhelming. I was very grateful to be at the birth of Tarynn and continue to be awed at all the changes she has gone through, although not surprised. Tarynn has always been a pioneer and one to push past boundaries. I would say the greatest change I've noticed is that Tarynn is at peace with life now. The sense of calmness is very present. She will always be close to my heart and I thank her for being a great teacher of life.

## Willow's Story (daughter, age 24)

I am the oldest. I have always been the responsible one, the one who compromises for the overall good, the one who has to impress all with her good grades and athletic abilities. I always saw myself as Daddy's girl -- never doing wrong or at least never wanting to do anything wrong to upset my parents. Sure, I'd mess up and do things every teenage girl eventually does, but I had always felt really close to my parents. My dad moved away when I was barely 16 years old and much of my life had begun to change.

I had started to notice a change in my dad long before I dared to say anything about it. My first fond memory was during my freshman year at college, when my dad had come down to help me move into my dorm room. He was setting up computer software and made a comment to my roommate and me about how fun it was to be hanging out "with just us girls." Many more clues began to arise when time after time I would see my dad and he would look more and more effeminate. His hair was getting longer, his body was thinning, and even his face seemed less dad-like and more woman-like.

Finally, a day or two before my seventeenth birthday my dad dropped two bombs on me. One, my parents were getting a divorce. Great. I wanted to die. Then, if that didn't hurt enough, my assumptions about him had been on the ball the whole time. He was in the process of becoming a full-fledged woman. Wow! What do you say to that? Cool, Dad, whatever makes you happy? No problem, I was hoping that would be the case? At 17, I barely knew myself and was looking for answers in response to the question "who am I?" I needed stability, and I had just lost my parents in two senses.

It's been a long road to travel in regard to my dad's gender switch, and there have been issues I've had to face that I really never thought I'd have to. My biggest one to conquer has been the feelings of anger that have stemmed from feeling that it all happened behind my back. I was not told about the change until it had already begun. Don't get me wrong; I love my dad no matter what his appearance is now or ever has been, but for me the biggest hurdle to jump was the feeling he didn't think I'd be on his side.

## Misty's Story (daughter, age 19)

When I first heard the news of my father deciding to change genders, I was beyond a doubt embarrassed, mortified, angry, sad, frightened, and countless other emotions. Why would he do this to me? What do I call him in public? What would I do if my friends saw me with him? Being around fourteen at the time, I opted to shove everything into the darkest corners of my mind. I assumed that if I left things alone, then my confusion would magically disappear. Well, four years have passed, I am nineteen now, and I have learned numerous ways to cope with this type of situation.

First, I only hurt myself more by avoiding my problems instead of facing them. Second, I had to acknowledge the idea that despite their drastic differences on the outside, they were still my parents underneath it all. Once that was out of the way, the rest was a piece of cake. Granted, it was incredibly awkward in public, but the more we did it, the more comfortable it got. Who cares if people stare? My motto is, it is better to be unique and have people stare, than to be the same and never be looked at.

My dad chose the name Tarynn, for his public name. The nice thing is that most of the time we can still use familiar terms of endearment such as Mom and Dad, when in the company of family and close friends. I still slip up every once in a while and say Dad in public, but that is okay. It is allowed. With respect to friends, if they are superficial enough to judge us based on our parent's change, then they aren't worth being around in the first place.

Lastly, I had to remember that this choice to change made him deeply happy. This happiness, like a halo of light, shines all around him. Formerly angry and frustrated, dad is now more friendly and open. As I traveled along this emotional rollercoaster, I had to keep in mind that we were not the only ones having this experience.

## Amber's Story (daughter, age 16)

Learning of my parents' divorce was hard enough on me. Then having to deal with something I thought was going to result in me having two moms. Well, lets just say, the ball flew into a whole new ballpark.

I will never forget the emotions and thoughts that taunted and baffled me during that time. I don't think I have EVER hated my dad so much. What would I call him? Did I have to see him looking this way? And a most commonly asked question: What did I do to deserve this? Well, you know what I did? Absolutely nothing! If a parent or family member decides to change their gender, it is not, of all people, anyone else's fault. It is something they had to do in order to lead a happy and fulfilling life. And amongst many other things I have learned while growing up, is to live with it. There are so much worse things going on in the world. We should not be too concerned as to whether to call him Mom or Dad instead of worrying about world hunger. Another thing is that this is what makes him happy, what makes his life worth living.

I know I would want my family's support if I made a life-altering change.   I still have a hard time being seen with my dad in public. After all, I am only 16 and I do face the everyday gossip and horrors that every high-schooler comes in contact with at some point in time. But I know now, and only after years of daily thoughts and ponders, that my dad still loves me and cares for me with all his heart and soul. Even if he doesn't look like everyone else or think like the rest, he is still the father that will walk me down the aisle at my wedding. He is still the dad I know and love. This situation can be one of the most difficult to face in the world, but finding the answers isn't difficult. We just have to look in our hearts and everything can be seen clearly.

### Tarynn's Ending (MTF father/mother)

To say that I am lucky to have the family that I do is to grossly understate how unique and special they all are. The truth is--I could not have done it without them. I love them all past where the numbers end, around and back again -- unconditionally!

# GOD BROKE THE MOLD
# WHEN HE MADE MY FATHER
## James Worgan

*I am 17, I am a junior at Granite Hills High School. I don't have a gender disorder. My hobbies are writing, drawing, building with Legos, playing video games. I have a learning disability, but am good at tactical thinking. I have three older sisters and a little niece.*

My experience has taught me that my dad has found a new lease on life. He has transformed into two people. One is still the man he's always been; however, the second is a woman.

The result is that we are spending more time together than we could have before because he was too worn out from the exertion of trying so hard to live like a man. When he returned to transition the chest pains stopped and his doctor took him off the heart medications by the end of the first month. He has so much more energy and interest in life now so we are able to do a lot more together than we could before. We play chess, go to the theater, and rent movies. Now we have talks about things in life without his getting angry. We have the same corny sense of humor and love for one another. I still call him Dad.

Since all this has happened, I have come up with the greatest conclusion I have ever thought of; for some reason it seems like my father is almost like a supreme being. He has the best of both worlds. On the one hand he has the caring ability of a woman and, on the other hand, the understanding of a male.

This is just another scenario you have to think about before you blame your fathers for their flukes of nature. If your father is a transsexual like mine, it is not your fault or your father's fault; he's just designed that way. This is my perspective. What will yours be?

There was one time when my dad had to go to the hospital because the stress put too much strain on his heart. I was so scared I was going to lose him. But here we are living together.

Now I am not so worried. Here's something to think about. Look inside yourself, and look at your father, and try to understand, as I do, why your father has to wear women's clothes. You might see a woman under those women's clothes. But don't trust your eyes; sometimes they can trick you. Look with your heart, because in your heart, he should still be your dad, nothing else, nothing less.

LAKE ROUNDERS
Sheila Mink

I see them,
But, so they see me,
I am wondering,
If they know I'm "I",
As they pass by,
Going 'round the lake,
Are they aware?
Do they think I'm fake?
Are they being nice?

# LOVE YOU, DADDY, NO MATTER WHAT
## Emma Rowe

*My name is Emma and I am fifteen years old. I have a younger brother, Alex, who is nine. I am in year eleven at school (my last year). In the future I am hoping to do a course at college, and then, hopefully, become an infant school teacher or a nursery nurse.*

Dear Mary,

I am a 15-year-old girl from England. A few months ago my father came out to us as a transsexual. To say we were surprised would be an understatement. I am coping generally fairly well, but I have problems with the thought of losing my father. I have told one or two close friends, including my boyfriend, and they have no problem with it, but all the same it is causing me a fair deal of worry. I have started to receive counseling at school, but it isn't really helping much as the counselor doesn't have much experience of this matter.

A couple of weeks ago we had a family crisis during which it became obvious that we were having problems. My dad promptly decided to stop his treatment because he could see how much we were hurting and he loves us so much that he couldn't carry on doing this to us. The next day, while he was at work, mum and I talked over what we would do, and decided that my dad should carry on with the treatment or it would tear him apart.

Just before I talked to Mum, I spent quite some time thinking, myself, and composed this letter to him. If you think it is suitable for inclusion in your book then please use it. I am enclosing it in this e-mail.

Yours,
Emma Rowe

Dear Dad:

I have thought a great deal about it all and I want to tell you, in this letter, what I find hard to say to your face.

I am trying hard to understand what you are going through. I suppose I could never understand completely, but I know for a fact what you must do, what you need to do. It will be very hard for me, but I think I may be able to come to terms with this (I am speaking on behalf of myself. Mum and I haven't talked properly as of yet.)

I am going to find it very hard to face you; it will be very difficult with you not being my dad. I love Mum dearly, but I suppose you could say I'm a daddy's girl. I have decided you should carry on with the treatment, because I know how important this is to you, and I want what is best for you. I will be able to get through this, with your love and support and with the help of family, friends and counsellors, but if you stopped treatment altogether -- will you get through?

You may be able to get help, but the feeling is always going to be there, do you want to go on living a lie? I believe you and I both know the answer.

I would also have to carry the guilt of not letting you have what you want, what you need. And as you said before, once a transsexual always a transsexual. All I want is for you to be happy, and seeing you happy, will make me happy.

Please, will you get me professional help to get me through this?

Love you always,
Emma

UPDATE

Emma emailed me some time ago that "Irene and Mum have divorced", but are friendly. Emma was working and taking classes toward her career goal. I greatly regret not being able to contact this brave young lady more recently. Ed.

# A DOUBLE-SPECIAL BROTHER
## Victoria Moon*

*When I first wrote this story, I was a graduate student studying bilingual special education. I am now pursuing a Ph.D. in Multicultural Special Education and hope to conduct diversity training for schools and also spend time with my two dogs. I have been involved in many groups advocating for human rights, sexual minorities, and the environment.*

Who am I?  For the purposes of this book I am a proud sister of a female-to-male transgendered individual.  Eight years my senior, my former sister was a strong female figure given a lot of parental responsibilities.   My mother left my father when I was three years old, deciding to raise her three kids on her own.

Mikeal, my brother (former sister) and the oldest, was left to watch us while Mom was at school or work.  He and I have always had a special relationship.  He is deaf, so he relied on me to be his ears when we were in public.  He has an amazing ability for reading my lips, so whenever he wanted to know what others were saying he would ask me.  Often I spoke to him using no voice; it was cool. However, now we use American Sign Language, which he learned after his high school graduation.

Since Mikeal's early years he had boyish tendencies and interests. He hated dolls and never wore dresses.  He loved cars and sports.  My mom was pretty supportive, thinking of him as a tomboy who would grow out of it.  My dad rejected him because of the communication breakdown.  I remember one time when my brother and I were at the playground.  The playground lady asked who the cute boy was with me and I told her that's not a boy, that's my sister!   On the way home my brother asked me what we said and I told him. He loved it.   In fact, he purposely bought boy clothes and tried to suppress his bust.

In the mid '80s, Mikeal went off to college and found himself in the punk scene.  There he could hide his femininity and

90

be accepted as "cool." He also came to terms with his attraction to women. When he told me he was a lesbian, I shrugged and said I knew. He couldn't believe how understanding I was, but I love my brother and neither his gender nor his sexual orientation will ever change that!

For many years Mikeal was considered a "butch lesbian." I know now he wasn't "butch" at all; he was a straight man trapped in a woman's body. As he went through lesbian relationships he realized his true identity. Women would say, "you're not gay," "you're different," or "you're not like other women." Finally, in his last lesbian relationship, his girlfriend brought up the notion that he might be transgendered. He thought, "Wow! Maybe that's why things are so hard for me in the lesbian community. Yeah, I do feel like a guy!" So, he began to research it.

That's when he ran into an old friend from high school. She was very supportive and actually was attracted to my brother. They began a long-distance relationship for a while. Now they live in the same town, but it is very difficult. Mikeal is a pre-op so he has difficulty passing, especially with the rising visibility of the lesbian/butch population. So his girlfriend often gets mislabeled as a lesbian. This upsets her because she loves my brother as a man. One day, after his identity is legally changed, they would like to settle and have a family.

Probably the biggest challenge Mikeal faces is that he is Deaf. The deaf community can be pretty closed-minded, so he constantly fears rejection. He works closely with the Deaf community as an historian of the language and culture. He is an educator in this community and highly respected. Because his girlfriend has already been mislabeled as a lesbian, they are unable to be together and present as a couple in the Deaf community. Really, it's horrible for them. Plus, to get the support he needs in order to go through this change, he needs an interpreter. It's ironic and very difficult, because he trained most of those same interpreters! They are thinking of moving because they are known and misunderstood by too many people there.

When I lived in the Southwest, Mikeal and his girlfriend came to visit me and I introduced them to other transgendered individuals. It was the first time he ever had face-to-face contact with another FtM. It was wonderful! It brought a sense of hope to both of them.

As I think back, when my brother first told me the news of his decision to become a man, I wasn't too shocked. I cried, though. I thought of my family and how they wouldn't accept him. I felt betrayed and tricked for all those years of identifying with HER. I had looked up to her as an empowered woman who didn't need to act feminine to be a woman. She broke all the rules and shocked people; she was strong and protective. I had thought of him as androgynous. This raises an interesting question about what is gender? A mere social construction of society??

Looking back, I realize how my now-brother has shaped my view on gender. I believe that we should each strive to balance gender within us. We should celebrate our femininity as well as our masculinity. Although I am quite feminine-looking, I embrace my own masculine side.

A good friend of mine introduced me to an amazing FtM woman, Patricia. She and I had long discussions and she connected me with PFLAG. At PFLAG, I met a wonderful mother of an FtM, who encouraged me to be more open with my mother. Being part of PFLAG and a transgendered support group really helped me deal with my own emotions and understand what my brother was and is going through.

My family has the general attitude that they will believe it when they see it. My mother and I talk often and she is in some denial. While she doesn't correct me when I refer to my brother as a "he" in conversation, she still refers to my brother as "she." My mom has become more comfortable with my brother's transition, however, and buys him cologne and clothes from the men's department. She feels that my brother is a part of her; she would never shut him out of her life.

For many years Mikeal was a male basher who taught me to be wary of men and their sexual intentions. For that I am thankful, but I do struggle to trust men and let myself go. When my brother came out to me my first question was, "Why do you want to be a man; you hate men!" He explained, with feeling, that he had bashed men because he was jealous. All his life he has walked in the shadows of men, only to be seen as a woman! He is cursed with large breasts, which still torture him every day of his life. One day, they will be gone and we will certainly celebrate!

UPDATE
Currently my brother is scheduled to begin hormone treatment this fall, to live officially as a man, and to send out letters to work, family, and friends. If all goes well, he will start reconstructive surgery at the end of his trial year living full-time as a man.

I swear never to be silent whenever and wherever human lives endure suffering and humiliation. We must always take sides. Neutrality helps the oppressor, never the victim. Silence encourages the tormentor, never the tormented. Sometimes we must interfere when human lives are endangered. When human dignity is in jeopardy, that place, at that moment, must become the center of the universe. -- Elie Wiesel, Holocaust survivor

* * *

Those who say something cannot be done should not interupt those who are doing it.
-- Chinese proverb ( Gary Bowen)

# ACCEPTANCE
## Elizabeth Vickery

*I graduated from Olivet College, married, have two daughters, and was widowed at age 36. I retired from Michigan Bell, married a second time at age 65 and was widowed again at age 79. A woman's club, poets society, aerobics and line dancing classes keep me active. I have five grandchildren and five great-grandchildren.*

My grandson used to be my granddaughter. It is at his suggestion that, at age 82, I write about my acceptance of the problems, developments, and changes of the beautiful baby whom I saw only minutes after she was born.

Acceptance can begin early in life. I was about sixteen when my mother brought home Radclyffe Hall's *The Well of Loneliness* for me to read. I had seen the picture of her in the Literary Digest and had tried to figure out if she was a man or a woman. My reaction to the book was sympathy for all the suffering the girl had endured. I thought her novel must have been at least somewhat autobiographical. My mother and I discussed her problems and feelings just as we had discussed *Candide* after I read that book.

Over the years I had talked to my aunt (my mother's sister), also, about all sorts of things. My mother's approach was mainly academic. My aunt's approach was more "down to earth." Between them, I learned a lot about understanding people, male and female.

Acceptance comes more easily when taught early. It also comes from being aware of the problems, changes and happenings over the years to someone you love -- to children or grandchildren, for instance. It can be handed down from generation to generation. My mother was born in 1888. I was born in 1915, my daughter in 1942, and my grandson in 1960. When my grandson first came out to her mother, her response was, "Aren't you the person I loved five minutes ago before I knew you were gay?" I was very proud of her for that.

Several years ago my granddaughter, which she was at that time, asked me to go with her to a gay bar. I was probably the only straight person there. We danced together as we always had around home. I liked the women who were her particular friends. I still correspond with one of them once or twice a year.

Humor can be a great help in acceptance, the humor of both people. When my grandson came to visit, sporting a beard, for a day or two it was a little strange, but the personality and voice were very familiar. Two incidents made it much easier. I ran into friends at a restaurant and introduced my grandson. When we got outdoors, he said with a big grin, "Congratulations, Grandma!" "What for?" He replied, "You only called me 'she' twice."

We were in a meat market and the lady waiting on him turned to me as if to say she'd be right with me and I said, "I'm with her." She looked at my grandson with an odd look, clearly meaning "Is that old lady wacko? Can't she see you're a man?" He and I managed to keep our faces straight until we got outside, where we became convulsed with laughter. It was especially therapeutic to us both because we both could see the humor in the situation and the knowing look she gave him. Acceptance can be easy and/or difficult, but as my mother used to say, "You can't help people by turning your back on them." You can learn to understand, as well as to love, them.

### UPDATE

Ron is recovering from an accident and surgery on his tailbone. He has a masters in social work and will soon return to his position working with the mentally ill. He also works in merchandise marketing, training employees. Best of all, he is happily married to a very wonderful (genetic) woman.

# MY NEW GRANDDAUGHTER
## Clela Fuller Morgan

*I raised four children, spent time as a missionary, and worked as a nurse. I have retired to Camron, Missouri, where I enjoy researching and writing for the local paper about the historical houses in the area.*

I used to have eight grandsons and two granddaughters and now have seven grandsons and three granddaughters; the most recent is the oldest. That might be difficult to explain, but not after you have met Danielle.

It has been a little more than a year since Evelyn told me that her 15-year-old son, Daniel, had revealed to her that he believed he was really a girl. Almost immediately I said, "He has always been a girl!"

You see, I have many memories of this special child. I remember the small boy of about three years who often sat on the arm of the couch combing and arranging his mother's long and curly hair. (He was still styling her hair years later.) That small boy liked to play with dolls and he saw some kind of value in a dismembered Barbie doll among the toys that I kept for visiting children. On his ninth birthday, his wish was for a doll with long hair and a pony with a long mane -- and the family fulfilled his wish. Several times he had me help him make clothes for his doll. He would pick out some material from the scrap box and together we would fashion clothes. His choice of cloth was always the bright shiny pieces.

In kindergarten, when he was getting settled in a new school, I asked how he liked it. He said, "It's beautiful! The colors are so pretty." I didn't understand that statement until I had an occasion to pick him up from school. Every schoolroom door around the big court was painted a different color -- pink, purple, green, blue, yellow -- so it was very colorful. He always described textures as well as colors whenever it was appropriate.

He never played any sports except when he was involved in acrobatic classes, which seemed to fit him naturally. He did

96

exceptionally well with that.

This little grandson was extremely loving. I always got a big hug when he came to visit, another when he left, and usually a time or two during the stay. He was also very sensitive to other people's feelings. He could tell when someone was not feeling well or was angry or uncomfortable.

At an age when most little boys were finding their friends from among the boys, his friends were girls. When he had a chance to take two or three friends on an outing on his birthday, he always picked girls, and this pattern of having girls for his close friends continued through junior high school.

Daniel was always close to his mother in ways that you would not expect of a son. They appeared to have such fun together. When he became old enough to be aware of his mother's clothes, he would advise her what to wear, and later she always took him along to pick out new clothes for her wardrobe. Two years ago his mother and I helped to host a bridal shower for a friend. Her son, then thirteen years old, arranged her hair. He used a small chignon of curls on the back of her head and, with a ribbon, blended it in with her own curls. The style was perfect with the flower print and lace of her dress. She was pretty as a picture, and Daniel appreciated and praised her beauty profusely.

He was the one in the family who would get the urge to clean and straighten the house, and would get after his brothers to put things away. As he started to think about his life work, he chose interior decorating. At one time I sent him a subscription to an interior decorating magazine, and I knew he liked to visit model homes to look at the furnishings.

Those of us close to this special child recognized that he was different, but had no clue as to the cause. He was very animated as he talked, with unusual movements of his hands and body. As I watched him walk, I sometimes thought, "Can't he walk like a boy? Doesn't he know he walks like a girl?" He knew, because his schoolmates teased him about his walk, and I know now that he couldn't do anything about it. Now we see those same movements and animation and feminine gait as perfect for a teenage girl.

The age at which Danielle made this drastic change was

unusual, for more often it is made much later in life. It wasn't a sudden idea, for Evelyn knew some months before the announcement that Daniel was emotionally upset. Some have wondered if a teenager of sixteen years should be making this important decision. Consider this question: At what point in life did you make the "decision" to be male or female?

What I think is commendable is that Evelyn immediately sought professional advice to assist Danielle to make the transition in the way that was best for her. This led to psychological testing, electrolysis, and hormone therapy--treatments which were uncomfortable and sometimes painful for Danielle. The fact that her brothers, cousins, aunts and uncles on both sides of her family were supportive, with one or two exceptions, is also commendable.

Some who have had qualms about getting acquainted with Danielle have had their doubts immediately swept away when they meet the beautiful, vivacious, outgoing young lady....I am so pleased to see her blossom scholastically and socially and her excitement about life is contagious. She has courageously faced the necessary difficulties and recognizes that the road ahead won't be easy, but she is up to it. Life sometimes uses strange ways to teach us tolerance and understanding of persons who have problems different from our own. How fortunate we are to be able to learn this lesson from Danielle!

### UPDATE

Danielle is 23, single, working full time, and as beautiful as ever. A joy to have around. Her father has finally come around, is trying to be accepting, and has let her back into his family. It took seven years. She never gave up hope. She is still looking for a good guy.

# PART V

## TRANSGENDERED PEOPLE TELL

## THEIR OWN STORIES

# Truths
## Walter Moyer

*I have been an active volunteer with several GLBT organizations, member of my church, and involved in spiritual journey work. I help churches to become "Welcoming Congregations" inclusive of GLBT through education. I also love the water, both to fish and walk on the beach, and recently moved to a houseboat to have a daily dose of the power of water.*

It has been said that spiritual awakening is not a destination but a road to be traveled. I believe that we are all spiritual beings and fellow travelers on that road. We are all on a journey that is spiritual as well as physical. Sharing the stories of our journey is one way we can encourage each other along the road, because although our stories are different, there are common threads of human experience that make us more alike than not. I hope that reading about my journey will help you be more aware of our common humanity than of our differences.

At 18 years old, a doctor looked me in the eye and said, "Here are your choices: you can stop drinking or you can be dead in six months." At 18, my body had already been damaged by 10 years of alcoholism. Since the age of eight I had been using alcohol to numb myself to the pain of growing up in an abusive family.

There are children who are born into communities of people who nurture and affirm their awareness of what is sacred within them. The rest of us grab hold of anyone or anything that might help us to survive. I was fortunate to have a godmother who recognized a child in distress, even if she could not let herself know what was happening in my family. I held on to her, and to a teacher who told me, "I know whatever is in there must really hurt. I wish I could help. I wish you could talk to me about it." But I did not have any words for what I was experiencing. Finally, I grabbed hold of alcohol. Drinking allowed my spirit to survive, but it left me with permanent physical damage.

At 18, the strategy that had helped to keep me alive was killing me. My choice was clear: to refuse treatment was to choose death. Yet my parents were opposed to my seeking treatment for alcoholism, on religious grounds, they said, though I suspect they were motivated by a fear that the family secrets would come out.

It was not an easy choice, as any misused child could tell you. Whatever I had suffered at the hands of these people, they were the only family I had.

I can look back on that moment and see that it was a turning point in my journey, a crucial fork in the road. I could go on living the lies of my family, or I could face the truth of who I was. I don't know where I found the courage to choose treatment. You might call it a human instinct for survival, or the call of the soul. Simply God was with me.

Newly sober, homeless and jobless. I took minimum wage jobs-cleaning toilets, stocking shelves, washing animal cages. Somehow I managed to live, going to work, going to 12-Step meetings, and counting every penny.

At this point in my journey, I met a fellow traveler who was a therapist. She recognized that emotionally I was a child in need of parenting, and she was able to give me the nurturing I had missed growing up. She helped me to find words for what I had experienced as a child. And she gently pushed me to acknowledge something else about myself: I was functionally illiterate. I had been able to hide this, and I was not gracious about her finding me out. She helped me to get past my shame, helped me to let go of the message I had been given that I was stupid. Many of our "therapy" sessions became reading lessons. I know I owe her a great deal, and I cannot bring myself to call it LUCK that she came into my life when she did. Being able to read opened up the world to me.

With the encouragement of my therapist and my friends, I enrolled in a class at a community college-just to improve my reading, I thought. But then I took one more class, then another, then two classes at a time. Eventually, I found myself completing community college with top honors and applying to universities. I graduated magna cum laude from a University with a degree in Accounting. I have specialized in taxation and have had my writings on taxation published in a professional journal. I taught accounting, bookkeeping, and taxation in various arenas. I started my own accounting practice and have expanded to include mortgage services. My professional accomplishments were part of a larger challenge: to come to terms with the truth about who I was.

When I had reached this level of security and success in my professional life, the road led me to another fellow traveler who would be my greatest teacher. She came into my life suddenly, when she was only six months old. She taught me about joy and laughter, about giving and receiving love. I had never changed a diaper until the day my daughter arrived, and I am grateful to friends who helped me with the practical problems of parenting.

I was able to work out of my home that first year, celebrating her progress and mine with astonishment. I loved parenting. Something of my own lost childhood was restored to me by being a child with her. At night, after reading the three books she chose, I sometimes read the tax code to her and put us both to sleep. I loved her with a depth and passion I did not know I was capable of. We both thrived.

My daughter was three when I lost her. It was the darkest period of my life. I was unable to work, unable to function, unable to remember why I should go on living. I felt stripped, naked, and emotionally raw. And yet, curled into a fetal position, emitting primal sounds of grief, I felt the presence of God and knew I was not alone. Again, there were friends and professionals to protect and support me. The road led me to a house at the beach, a setting so therapeutic I am still trying to figure out how to write it off as a medical expense. Slowly, slowly, I learned to live with my loss. I can't say that I have recovered from it. Seven years later, my arms still ache to hold her one more time.

Losing my daughter put many things in a new perspective for me. Getting stuck in traffic or having a business deal fall through are pretty minor incidents on the road of life compared to losing a child. Other things became MORE important: telling friends you love them, thanking someone for a kindness, celebrating each moment you have with loved ones.

Losing my daughter also made the pretenses of my life unbearable. It was time for me to face up to the rest of who I was. I spent many hours walking on the beach, having long conversations with myself and with God. And what I realized was that I was still living one lie, and I could not go on. I had been born in a female body, but I knew in my heart, in my very bones, that I was male. I had a good life and a successful practice living as a female. In a sense, I was hiding in the persona of a woman. But I knew that I could not continue to fool the world, betraying my knowledge of who I am. Choosing to live as a man would mean living truthfully, transparently, -- revealed to the world as who I truly am.

I always knew I was male. As a child, I thought the rest of the world would eventually realize their mistake and stop trying to make me a girl. I thought doctors would recognize the mistake and correct it like any other birth defect. As an adult, I was told that I was not a male but a lesbian, and I tried hard to accept this. But finally, after losing my daughter, there seemed to be no reason to pretend anymore.

But it took a lot of walking on the beach to come to that choice. I worried about the expense, about the physical risk and pain of surgery. I worried about losing my practice, about losing my friends, about what people would say. I worried about losing the protective mask I hid behind. Finally, when I could be truly honest with myself--not only about who I was, but about what I had done, mistakes I had made, people I had hurt--then I was able to walk with a new, clear awareness of the presence of God in me and around me. And I was no longer afraid. I knew what I had to do.

Ultimately, it came down to this. The lie was costing me too much. At 18, I had chosen to reject the lie that I was a healthy member of a happy, functional family, when I was not. Then I chose to face the lie that I could read, when I could not. And I had spent my adult life systematically letting go of the lies I had been told about myself as a child. Now this most basic fact about who I am demanded to be acknowledged. I am a man, and I now had the opportunity to make my outsides match my insides. I had the opportunity to present myself to the world as who I truly am.

Walking on the beach, I came to a new understanding of my humanity: that I was only a grain of sand in the wide universe, that my struggles were insignificant from the cosmic view. And yet the choices I made were of the greatest importance, because the condition of the world is a product of the accumulated choices that all of us make.

Today I am legally male. My name is Walter Wilson Boone-Moyer, a name I chose as a way of claiming my heritage as a man descended from men. One of those men was James Boone, my maternal grandfather, who was part Native American. He was one of our family secrets because it was a matter of shame that he was not "white". Taking his name is another way that I can refute the lie, drop the pretense, and be who I am.

Some of the fears I had about transitioning were valid: I did lose some clients and some old friends who could not accept my truth. Since transitioning, I find that I am able to relate to people with an ease and freedom I never knew. A trans friend says it is like having the emotional elevator freed to go down to the basement instead of being stuck at the top two floors. Since transitioning, I find that my commitment to social justice is stronger; my desire to relieve others' suffering is more compelling.

Some of you may have trouble understanding how all of this is part of my spiritual journey. That is the sense of fraudulence I had in my life. There is a heavy spiritual price to pay for living such a lie, even if it is forced on you.

I think that leading an authentic life, a transparent life, without pretense, is a challenge for any human being. There is enormous pressure to hide our faults and pretend to fit into our family's dream, or society's prescribed role, for us. One principle I live by is to affirm the inherent worth and dignity of every person. To do this for others, we must begin by knowing ourselves, all our warts and blemishes, and affirming that even in the harshest light of self-knowledge, we are worthy.

In connection with my church I had a rites-of-passage service. I found it was not about me, but about the transforming power of truth in all of our lives.

A principle I try to activate in my life is to encourage another's spiritual growth -- "to give courage" to someone or "to give heart" to someone, and I hope that something you have read here has done that for you. I hope you have been reflecting on your own path, on the turning points, on the teachers you have encountered along the way, on the moments when the presence of God broke through. Thank you for honoring my story as I honor yours.

# IRENE'S STORY
## Irene Preiss

*I hold BA and MA degrees in Education, retired as a Naval officer, and am the author of "Fixed for Life." (See Amazon.com) Former occupations include textbook editor, marketing communications, and industrial engineer. My "pasture time" these days in Puget Sound is devoted to communications with new transwomen, reading mystery novels, and part-time employment as a writer for a local game-simulation company.*

I look back over the last 74 years and think I have had quite a ride on this planet. I was born a boy, and now I am an old lady. Let me tell you what happened.

My childhood was pretty good. My mother and father cared very much for my brother and me. I think I was about seven or eight when I began to sense that I should have been a girl. No one ever talked about boys becoming girls, so I just assumed it could never happen, and that I must be crazy or a sissy. I was not stupid enough to tell anyone. I always played with boy toys, and boy games. I liked endurance-demanding sports like water polo and swimming. The feeling about being a girl grew within me. Fantasies began. Imaginary social settings where I would suddenly appear as a girl and everyone would be amazed at how good I looked. Then I would think how wrong it was to think like that.

In high school I discovered girls. I liked being a boy with a girl. Hugging and kissing and holding hands were really big stuff. My body's reaction to such delights was overwhelmingly male. I liked being the boy, but I also wanted to be a girl. Not to be a girl with a boy, but just to be one of the girls. I was really confused about all of that. Who wouldn't be?

In 1945 I joined the Navy. I thought I could become a man and be rid of the desire to be a girl. Boot camp was the toughest physical trial I ever had. I proved to myself that I could be a real man. That was important for me to learn. I still wanted to see if I could be a girl, dammit.

The next three years were spent at sea. All of that time was in the Orient. On liberty, we would frequent brothels and other places of interest to young sailors. I was discharged in 1949, enlisted in the Naval Reserve, and started college. After a year, I was recalled to active duty for the Korean conflict. I asked a young lady to marry me. I had the secret hope that a good marriage would put an end to my fantasies.

Two weeks after the honeymoon, I asked if I could try on her nightgown. We really loved each other, but the desire to pursue female things was still with me. She was stunned and angry. She thought I was homosexual. I needed her support, but she needed a husband who behaved like a man. I shipped out for Korean waters. A year later, I was transferred from the destroyer to a cruiser in Portsmouth, VA. Helen came to visit me. We rented an apartment, made lots of love, and vowed to fight for the marriage.

In 1952 I returned to college and Helen became pregnant. Another big event that year was the news of Christine Jorgensen. The media regarded her sex-change surgery as a scandal --- I regarded it as hope. My heart leaped with joy that someone was able to accomplish it, but I could not see it for me. I just wanted to be able to appear in public as a woman ... once in a while. So why was I so excited about Christine's good fortune?

By 1955 I had my degree, a teaching credential, a job, a house, and two sons. I was "getting there" in terms of living the ideal life. Helen was continually unhappy with me. I was continually disappointed in her for not supporting me. I did all the husband stuff and all the dad stuff. I even participated in the production of a third son. I did all the things I was supposed to do, but could not even try on women's clothing. I never asked for that desire, but it surely was there. And growing.

After 22 years of marriage, I asked for a divorce. I was dealing with a lot of emotional stress and beginning to manifest physical abnormalities as well. I had tried to live up to my responsibilities as a husband and father. Those moral lessons learned throughout childhood were governing my actions, but my emotions said to stop it. My sons were maturing and I thought I could permit myself to leave that home and still have some self-respect.

I had been to psychologists, but in the 1960s they knew nothing about my condition. I had personal counseling from church people. Only general guidelines were offered. One of them suggested that perhaps my soul (or core) was trying to tell me something. At the time, that did not seem useful. Not then, anyway.

I rented an apartment, continued in my job as a school administrator, but spent evenings and weekends dressing up and experimenting with cosmetics. Wow! I felt as though I was doing something right, in general, but I was clumsy. I went to a modeling school. They were very sympathetic to my needs, and through them I learned of the Gender Dysphoria Clinic at Stanford University Hospital. I made an appointment for screening. Was I really a woman inside or not? The results said the female gender predominates in me. At last, a medical and psychological team had confirmed the feelings I had. I was on a track to see how far I could go as a woman and if I wanted to be a woman.

I met Annie at work and fell in love. I was torn apart by that realization. We dated a few times before I told her about my predicament. She was not especially concerned as long as she did not have to participate in my explorations. Annie and I decided to try living together as a family with her three daughters. We agreed to a one-year trial period. That went well, but I needed some times out to experiment on a weekend now and then. By the end of that year, I had an opportunity to work as Irene, my chosen name. That meant leaving Annie and her girls. The editorial job was wonderful, and I made lots of women friends at work. The job lasted about six months.

My next job was as a male. That one lasted a year. After that, another one-year job for Irene. Whenever I was male, I could live with Annie. Otherwise, Irene lived alone. I marvel at Annie's resiliency. We were married in 1979.

In the spring of 1988, I knew I had to spend the rest of my days as Irene. I had done a considerable amount of reading and thinking over those years, and I knew that my purpose in life required that I live it as Irene. It was like "a calling." I asked Annie if she would stay with me, but she said no. Another divorce. I moved to another state and restarted life with a clean slate. I had all of my documents changed to my new name and gender. It took about five months to get a job teaching basic skills to sailors. I applied for gender reassignment surgery and had that done in early 1990. I was able to work as stealth -- the term for passing as a woman without telling anyone. I was later promoted to administrative posts, and then retired from that college job at age 69. I was tired.

I wrote my memoir, partly to help me understand myself, and partly to help others understand what this transgender thing is about. I wanted to be of service to others like me. While I was seeking a publisher, something called the Internet was invented. Within a few years, there was an explosion of information on transgenderism and many thousands of men finding others like themselves, and finding all kinds of information from the research communities. I joined the net.

What is left of my life is being devoted to helping my younger sisters in any way I can. I have been active in PFLAG and a few local transgender organizations. I often meet with beginners for lunch. I am here to serve others, and find that my life is sweet.

\* \* \*

Only two things are infinite, the universe and human stupidity, and I'm not sure about the former.

The world is a dangerous place to live, not because of the people who are evil, but because of the people who don't do anything about it.     --both Albert Einstein  (Gabi Clayton)

\* \* \*

I've come to realize that many people realize what I'm doing, so I'm just going to be me.   - Sheila Mink

# WHAT MATTERS NOW?
## Janice J. Carney

*I am 51 now. I live for my night walks and day swims at The Beaches. I recently found a passion for writing poems and short stories. Reading, dancing and banging my drum are my other hobbies.*

### Prologue

When I was born in 1950, the doctor declared I was a boy. I knew early on that I was not, but it was not until my mid-forties that a doctor confirmed that fact. He said I had a hormonal imbalance. After years of being told it was "all in my head," I finally learned I could balance my hormones and lead a "normal" life. I soon started hormonal treatment and the journey to wholeness. In 2001 I had a form of rebirth through intersex surgery (often called sexual reassignment surgery) and my birth certificate was changed to list both my current name and proper sex.

I begin with this glow, a feeling of completeness. For the first time in my life, my body, my soul, my spirit, and my mind are one. But what matters now? My life goes on. I am still the loving parent of three beautiful children. My 20-year-old son totally accepts my newfound bliss. Shaun has told me, "Dad, whatever you are doing, it is good. You smile now, you are sober, and you are not nervous and angry all the time."

My two young daughters are still my main concern. They mean so much to me. Two weeks before my surgery I took them aside separately, and tried to get them to open up to me. I have been out of their house for over two years now. For a year and a half another person has been sleeping with my wife.

What matters now? I have this miracle: A chance through surgery to put my life-long nightmare to an end. Am I being selfish? Yet, my daughters' well-being is what matters now.

I tell my loving Melissa that I am still her father. I always will be. She has spent the last three years watching her father's rebirth as a women. Every Wednesday night I take them out; I have not missed one yet.

What matters now? For the last time I am letting my babies control me, giving them more power then I should. I trust my years of home schooling them have made them wise. The scars from my service in Viet Nam still haunt me; yet that service-connected disability gave me an income that allowed me to be home with my babies.

I cannot have this surgery, if in any way it will come between us, I tell my loving Melissa. She smiles, gazing into my tearful eyes. "Dad," she says, " I know you love me. I know you are happy, and that is all that I need to know." "You know I would go back for you," I whisper. She says, "Back to being sad, drunk, and angry all the time." We finish our burgers and shakes. This is all that matters now.

Now I ask my younger daughter the same question. I invite my little computer expert over to my apartment to work on my website, "I WAS ALWAYS ME." It is not long before she spills out that Melissa has told her about my upcoming surgery, and of my question to her.

What matters now? "You matter now," I assure her. Jeanette, who from day one has been crying out, "I want my dad back," now looks at me with a smile. She is just twelve years old and a spitting image of me with curly hair and big blue eyes behind her glasses.

With the wisdom of many more years then she has, she says, " I know you are my dad, and I know you love me. I know you will still be my dad even after the surgery." We talk about a movie she saw called "The Adventures of Sebastian Cole". I reassure her that it was just a movie. In real life no one dies from intersex surgery.

She gives me a big hug! This is all that matters now!

### Epilogue

My voice is my last gender wall; I have torn down all the other gender walls. Those short manly haircuts have been replaced with long flowing, curly, touched up hair. That flat hairy chest replaced, thanks to hormones, with small perky breasts. That huge beer gut is gone. Thank the Goddesses! My fat mass has shifted, my hips have emerged. Yes that wall of gender denial has been torn down.

My face, now soft and hairless, is smiling; now the life-long sadness gone. My hands were one of those walls, perpetually dirty and callused, a part of the gender wall now clean, soft with long painted nails. My legs, once hairy and always hidden under my pants, now are hairless, soft and shapely. They now are tanned from the exposure to the sun; another gender wall torn down.

Oh, how I have torn down all those gender walls right down to my feet, yes, my feet! My feet, too, are usually naked in the Florida sun, showing off my tastes in toenail coloring! My gender walls-- Oh, how they have all been torn down!

Well, all but one. My Voice, MY VOICE. This deep voice, this vocal expression that is part of me. I keep this wall; I keep this wall. I have said it is the last trait of my children's father. I have said that I am too lazy to do voice exercises. My child has cried, "Don't change your voice; it's the last of my father!" My voice is me; I just need to keep some of me! My last gender wall, I keep it up. I really do not know why.

* * *

At the time when I was making the decision to transition, and starting to tell some friends what was about to happen, I was teaching private flute students full time. I was sharing a tiny studio in a large music store with a friend and "flute colleague" whom I had known for some years and performed with regularly. I had been looking for a good time to tell this friend about my decision to transition, and was a bit anxious about it since I had no idea how she felt about such things.

One day when we were both there, I decided this was the right moment. We went into the studio, closed the door and I spilled the beans. After she picked her jaw up off the floor, she asked some thoughtful questions and I gave some honest answers. By the end of the half hour she said, "Well, you'll still be you. I mean, it's not like you're becoming a bassoonist or something."

--Dean Allen*

112

# GIRL AMONGST BOYS
## Joshua Bastian Cole

*I was raised in New Jersey and have one younger brother. I am a recent Theatre and Dance graduate of James Madison University where I was involved with Harmony, JMU Freethinkers, Army ROTC, and Varsity Fencing. I plan to attend graduate school at the University of Texas at Austin for Queer Theory and Performance.*

It is a difficult thing to pinpoint at exactly what moments in my life, I began displaying the behaviors of some given label. I know that I felt different from the girls in my preschool. I liked playing with boys, and they liked me because I was more like them than other girls. I knew I was a girl, though. So, I was labeled a "tomboy"; I was a girl amongst boys. I liked boys; I got along with them and I wanted to look like them.

I was lucky to have hand-me-downs from older boy cousins, and I was lucky to have a mom who let me wear them. She gave up trying to put me in a dress for temple because I cried so much about it. She would not give me boy dress-up clothes, but just left me with a baby sitter, which is, of course, a million times better than being forced into a dress.

Although I grew up as a tomboy, I was socialized into mixed environments. I played Little League baseball and soccer, but I also took ballet and acrobatics, and I joined the Girl Scouts. I was an androgynous kid, and I remember getting funny looks when I wore my ballet attire or bathing suits, because people thought I was a boy. It was embarrassing to be mistaken as a boy in front of my parents, but deep down, I liked it.

When I was a kid it was acceptable to wear boys' clothes and play Little League. By middle school it was awkward, and by high school, it was weird and basically unacceptable. All of the other girls were becoming women, and I did not really want to. I reluctantly began wearing women's clothes and growing out my hair.

In high school, I began to notice attractions toward other girls, but I quickly dismissed them because it was, in my head, "gross," "wrong," and "perverted." I had several boyfriends, but they all ended up being more like buddies to me, just like my early childhood. I wanted to be "one of the guys," but again, I was a girl amongst boys. I was jealous of their haircuts and their clothes and their bodies, but I quickly dismissed these thoughts.

My college was even more homogenous, and it was becoming harder to believe I was like the young women around me. I believed that if I could find a boyfriend, everything would be "normal," but in the middle of my freshman year, I had an undeniable crush on a girl. I thought it must mean I was bisexual, because I still had a fascination with boys, a fascination that I mistook for attraction.

I had a girlfriend for a year. My girlfriend, Laura, told me that she was attracted to my boyish aura. She was attracted to androgyny. I was disgusted by the idea. I did not want to be an androgynous boyish girl. I tried hard to be a girlish girl, but it just did not work anymore. Laura encouraged me to find the boy in my head she knew was there. I knew it, too, but I absolutely denied it, and it made me miserable.

After we broke up, I saw the movie we had been meaning to see all year, Boys Don't Cry, about Brandon Teena. I respected Brandon for being able to live as a man, something I could not yet tell myself I wanted to do. I thought Brandon and I were alone in the world, and Brandon was murdered!

Soon after seeing the movie, I changed my name from Belinda to Bailey, but did not tell very many people. I still did not know why, really.

In August, I made a friend named Jessie. We were just chatting, but Jessie ended up introducing me to transgender, a word I had not heard. Jessie explained it to me, and also introduced me to some transboys my age. I was shocked, but also extremely relieved. I was not alone in the world, and this was who I was, just like these other college-aged females living as boys.

I talked online with some FTMs and asked a lot of questions. I was not sure I wanted to live full-time as a male, and I definitely was not sure about medical transition. In talking to other FTMs, I came out as trans, but I was identifying as gender neutral, and using the name Bailey.

In November, I met some of the guys in person. It was great. We all belonged with each other, and there was nothing to be embarrassed about. It was here that I met my friend, Michael. He was a few months into his medical transition. People looked at me, and saw "lesbian," but with Michael, you could only see "boy." I wanted that. I came out as an FTM.

In February, we all met again at the True Spirit Conference, a national FTM conference. I was amazed at all of the guys on testosterone, and how masculine their bodies and voices were. I was jealous. I changed my name from Bailey to Joshua, a name my mother liked. I wanted to be a boy, and I knew that I needed a more obviously masculine name. So now people started to assume I was a lesbian named Josh, but I was getting closer.

I did gender therapy all spring, and when I came back to school in fall for my senior year, my name was legalized. At the end of October, I started low-dose testosterone, a decision I had made in therapy, and soon came out as a femme boy. I realized that I did not want to go full-force into living as a male. I wanted to hold on to my queer identity, and to explore my femme identity, but I definitely wanted testosterone. After adjusting my dosage, my voice dropped, and my body started to change.

I graduated from college and moved out on my own. For the first time, I was really passing. It was a weird thing to get used to, though. People assumed I was male, even after I started talking.

My voice has become a baritone, and my face has squared off. It is still strange to have people assume I am male. I want that, I know, but I also want to be out as trans. Since it does not come up in conversation, I am unintentionally stealth. At work, people I'm with think I am a young-looking guy.

Because I am a femme guy, people assume I am gay, and I like that. Still, it makes me a little sad when lesbians look past me because they think I am a guy. It is hard to give up all of my old female identity.

I am attracted to other FTMs, and those relationships tend to be the most successful. I am attracted to their masculinity and their female bodies. Even if I end up with a woman, our relationship will still be queer.

It can be frustrating to have people make assumptions about my past, about a boy childhood I did not have, and about who I am now. I know what it is like to be a woman. I know things that biological men will never know. But I wanted testosterone so that my body, my face and my voice would match the person in my head. My friend, Michael, put it so well when he said, "I can look in the mirror, and see myself."

I know who I am, and who I was. I remember.

We have one son who had leukemia, another son who was a lesbian and came out a second time as a transsexual, and a straight, healthy daughter -- whom we love anyway. :-)    MMB

# BECOMING WHOLE AT LAST
## Just Ashleigh*

*Nearing retirement in a number of years from a State affiliate of the Federal Department of Labor, I have become a Benedictine Oblate in the Catholic Apostolic Church in North America. As I complete my transition, I am preparing to work with youth who are GLBT, with emphasis on those who are experiencing what I am going through. I hope to obtain monastic status and, eventually, become a priest.*

I don't recall the month or year this happened, but we were living on the outskirts of town. My experience with crossdressing and, eventually, gender transition began innocently enough when I found one of my sister's bathing suits. It was a one-piece light green stretch suit. Over the months after that, I had tried on several one-piece sunsuits which tied on the shoulders. I would wear these to bed instead of pajamas.

Then on October 18th, 1998 at the age of 52, I told my dad what was bothering me. "I want to begin the process of becoming your daughter instead of your son." His response was that he would support me in whatever I did, but that he wanted me to think long and hard about it. I didn't know how to explain to him that it's not an overnight thing. I had already been thinking long and hard!

I'm not quite sure why I was attracted to the name Kimberly, but my second name, Ashleigh, came from a story I found on the Internet. Entitled "Cousins", by Karen Elizabeth L, they were always getting in trouble because of misbehavior. I felt that, because of my feelings and the need to be Kimberly, I was misbehaving.

Dad died on July 28, 1999. I moved out of the house and accepted an offer to begin the ministry process. When I first came to the western part of the state, it was to assist at Mass at an assisted living facility. I had been assured that the parish would accept my transition. Later I moved into my own apartment. I have two wonderful Bishops who know what's going on and are very helpful.

On October 22, 1999 Brandi, the lady who interviewed me for membership in the support group, died unexpectedly. I had a hard day at work the day of the viewing. In addition, my supervisor at work came in unexpectedly when I was leaning over the computer. Since I was wearing women's underclothes, but not out at work, I was afraid that he might have seen the outline of my bra, something I didn't want him to see. (My work was in the Tax Collection Unit of a state affiliate of the Federal Government) I walked into his office and asked for a meeting in the conference room with him and his supervisor. I outed myself to both of them and gave permission for the assistant supervisor of the unit to be informed as well. I also obtained and provided them with reference materials to read about what I was going through. They both took it well and created a supportive atmosphere.

Dad warned me about my choice of underwear. "What if you get into an accident?" Well, I did! Coming home from a union steward's training session, one Saturday, while crossing the main highway, my Honda was totaled by a southbound driver running a red light. I was transported by ambulance as a precaution. I learned how patients feel when being removed from a vehicle and slid onto a backboard. It's scary! I remember being afraid that I was going to fall off, but more afraid of being undressed. Luckily I never was.

Several days later, I was going home when hurricane Floyd hit. Without remembering that the northern entrance to where I live sometimes floods in bad weather, I drove right into the flooded part of the road in the dark and the car filled with water. I was rescued by the fire company, where I was a member, for the second time in ten days. The dispatcher that night was one of our members and kept me on the cell phone trying to calm me down. By the time I was pulled out of the vehicle, there was only one to one and a half inches of air space in the car. They took off my wet outer clothes and saw the lingerie. I simply explained that I was transitioning. Big deal! Patient Confidentiality. But the crew inside the back was something else -- the former EMS

(Emergency Medical Services) Captain, the current EMS Captain and the incoming EMS Captain all learned my secret, but nothing happened. The rest of the company had no knowledge of what took place.

While in the western part of the state, I joined a fire department there. I spent a number of Friday nights sleeping with my bra showing through my blouse only to put on a sweater when we got a call or it was time to get up. I wore even more lingerie the weekends I went to a training class in that area. I talked to the former president of the company and apparently none of them realized that I was transitioning at the time.

After a couple of poor responses, I finally found the counselor I am now working with. I started with him in June of 2001 and in October was approved for Hormone Replacement Therapy and began that as my Christmas present. We continue to get along great!

My supervisor and I had talks from time to time when I needed someone to talk to. In a spirit of learning, while we were talking about clothes, he asked about lingerie. I responded, "Where have you been? I've been wearing lingerie to work for the last ten to fifteen years." And I had. I later realized that it may have been closer to thirty years.

In preparation for progress as a Benedictine, I outted myself over the Internet to the Benedictine members of my monastery and told them what was happening. We're not cloistered so we all live in different places.

I moved back to the eastern part of the state and joined PFLAG, where one of my first events was World Aids Day. As Kimberly, I made my first public appearance in the county.

I've been on hormones for eight months now and have not only transitioned on the job, but have become Kimberly full time. What was exciting was toward the end of May at our headquarters during a Labor Management Committee meeting when I ran into someone I hadn't seen in a while. We went back into the conference room and began talking. Then looking at me she asked, "Are you growing breasts?" We had a nice talk and I told her what was going on. About a month later, I had stepped out into the hall and met the trainer that gives a series of courses I'm taking. Her mouth fell wide open when she saw me. We talked before the last class this month and she alerted the Assistant Secretary that I was going through some changes. The Benedictines have approved my new name, and I am in the process of updating other papers as well.

I am looking forward to October 1st, when I anticipate further advancement -- when I go with my lawyer to court for my legal name change and I receive the official date to begin the Real Life Experience.

No person is your friend (or kin) who demands your silence, or denies your right to grow and be perceived as fully blossomed as you were intended. Or who belittles in any fashion the gifts you labor so to bring into the world.      -- Alice Walker

# JASMYN
## Michelona Delonta

*I was raised in Roanoke, VA, moving to New York City in 1994. I returned to Roanoke, which is home to me, and have been clean and sober for two years. I have worked as a hairdresser and in store management, and am in a loving relationship.*

As a child I have fond memories of being alone, playing school with imaginary friends or playing beauty salon with my mother on the living room floor.

I never became a third grade teacher like I always told the grown-ups I wanted to be whenever asked that well-anticipated question, "What do you want to be when you grow up?"   I completed   900 hours of academic time as a hairdresser before dropping out to pursue other adventures.   The road that I chose to take would be a life's lesson and a far deadlier cry in an uncaring, unprotective, lonely world.   On the paths that I took, I sought acceptance, the need for everyone to like me, and the over-need for attention. These were the things that I was not achieving to this point from family members and so-called friends.

Prostitute, escort (a fancier name  for selling your body), drug addict and a rap sheet of petty larceny, attempted "malicious wounding and property/vehicle damage" became my titles and much more of a life's choice than a lifestyle.

In 1997 I was convicted on an attempted  wounding and property damage, violation of probation and sentenced into the desolate Virginia Department of Corrections for a term of twenty-two months.

Only 21 years old and a male-to-female transsexual, I had breasts from hormonal therapy that I took since 1994, and also some silicone injections to enhance other feminine aspects of my face and body.

As I followed behind to the cell that awaited me, a holler went through the prison's corridor from a deputy anouncing that "new meat" was on the compound.        Inmates screaming and

121

shouting, placing bids and assuring other inmates that I would belong to them, filled my ears.   Much like a pimp with his whore, I was told that I would "work" for one man to pay off his gambling debts; another told me that I had only a few days to decide that I was his, or he would take further action.

I kept proclaiming that I just wanted to do my time alone. I was already fresh out of a long-term relationship prior to getting incarcerated and very scared of coming back home with HIV or Hepatitis C that were prevalent in the prison compound.

One inmate in particular had contacts among prisoners and guards to get me moved to his dormitory. He would tell me he loved me and how he was going to take care of me, now that I was his girl! He began to push himself on me and, as I fought back, others witnessed me hit him with a chair. He was called names that normally I was called, such as a "punt", a "gump", etc.

Later that week,  as I was walking  in the prison's recreational yard, I felt a sharp pain on the back of my head, blood flowed down my face though I was still standing.  As I turned around an aluminum baseball bat struck my forehead, my jaw, my left hand and elbow as I tried to block the swings; I slid, bloody and crying, down a fence.

Inmates crowded around, even other guards stood looking on.  One inmate picked me up in his ams, as my own blood became his, and carried me to a cement bench.  I fought for my life, never going unconscious, but  the pain made me I  wish I would have. Blood drained into the back of my throat as I prayed to God to let me live.

I was transported to a major hospital an hour away where I was treated for severe head and maleo-facial traumas.  I required 32 stitches in my forehead and 22 staples in the back of my head;  I also had a shattered elbow and hand, and a broken jaw and teeth.

Showing no sympathy, the warden of the prison and other head officals of the DOC exclaimed that it was my own fault for "being the way you are."

The healing process took what seemed like forever. Today the physical scars have  healed, but the continued remembrance of that day that nearly cost me my life due to my being a transsexual woman incarcerated in an all-male institution, improperly classified or attended to, still flourish in my thoughts.

The fight will never be over, but like a butterfly I, too, look forward to gaining my wings so I can fly.

All you need is Love to support Equality and Justice for ALL. When you fail to support equality and justice for all, you have failed as a person. -- Michael J. Golojuch, Jr.

# FROM FEMALE TO NOT-FEMALE
## Reid Vanderburgh

*I am a transman and psychotherapist living in Portland, Oregon. I received an MA in Counseling Psychology in 2001. The focus of my practice is helping people cope with major life transformative events, including transition, and facilitating groups for transgendered and their family members. I can be reached through the editor.*

I was 39 years old, living as a lesbian, when I first realized I'd probably be happier living as a guy. I did not take kindly to this realization, for several reasons. First, I had quite a life built up in the Portland (Oregon) lesbian community. I was a founding member of nine years' standing of the Portland Lesbian Choir, and leaving that group was not on my horizon.

Second, I had a family of choice with whom my bonds were stronger than those with my biological family. All were lesbians. All were fellow choir members, or members of my mixed chorus, Bridges Vocal Ensemble. Or members of both. Queer folks find family as we are able, and often the bonds forged through living in a hostile society are stronger than the bonds of blood connection. I was scared of my realization -- if I became a man, would I lose my family of choice?

Finally, I had a negative reaction to the idea of being trans because I had absorbed the mainstream belief that being trans was weird, sick and perverted. Whenever I did see someone obviously trans, I felt uneasy and off-balance, as if I was in the presence of someone who was psychotic, or not fully human. I had some vague equation of "transsexual" and "drag queen" as synonymous, which of course had made it impossible for me to recognize myself as a transsexual earlier in my life. I've loathed feminine clothing for as long as I can remember, which is hardly the attitude of a drag queen!

I'd never had conscious fantasies about being male. I had just never felt completely at home in my skin as a female, causing a low-grade anxiety and depression that was growing steadily as I aged. I hated women's bathrooms. I did not like introducing myself to others, as my former name was highly feminine. I avoided describing myself as a lesbian, and felt vaguely uncomfortable referring to myself as a woman. I had never visited an ob/gyn in my life. I was full of contradictions and felt an enigma to myself --not an easy life for a Virgo.

I would probably still be living in denial had my then-partner not come out to me in the spring of 1995, telling me one night, "I've always felt like a man inside." This effectively held a mirror to my soul. I could no longer ignore what I saw there, but was not prepared to face it. The effect was rather like a badly done substance abuse intervention. Because of the negative attitudes I'd internalized about what it meant to be trans, I had a difficult time feeling okay about the concept of going through female-to-male transition.

Then one day a bisexual friend said to me, with some envy in her voice, "What a gift, to be able to live as both sexes in one lifetime." This one phrase reframed the experience for me, for the first time putting a positive spin on the concept of being trans. Nowhere else had I encountered a positive interpretation of what it might mean to be trans. I moved forward with a great deal more confidence and excitement at the possibilities inherent in the unexpected opportunity life had presented me.

I postponed my physical transition for nearly two years, waiting for the Portland Lesbian Choir to record its first CD. I spent those two years in gender limbo-land, being seen primarily as male in my undergrad classes at Portland State University (unless I opened my mouth to speak), being seen as in transition at work, and being seen as a lesbian during choir rehearsals. I felt the split keenly, never being able to quite integrate these various aspects of my life into one cohesive whole, despite the fact that I came out to everyone who was important to me. Transition cannot be done in the closet.

Once I began hormones and had top surgery, life became much simpler, as my former lesbian life faded away gradually. However, what I found is that I did not become more male in my outlook on life. I became fully male in appearance, while retaining many of the values I'd learned in the lesbian community. I did not feel much more comfortable calling myself a man than I had calling myself a woman, or a lesbian, though I felt fine calling myself a guy and definitely felt more comfortable in my own skin. I did not lose my lesbian family of choice, and found those friendships have retained their original intimacy. If anything, they are deeper than ever, as I am more centered and thus more capable of truly intimate relationships.

I gradually came to realize that I had not transitioned from female to male. I had transitioned from female to not female. In the ensuing years, I have come to agree with Kate Bornstein, a transwoman writer and performer, who stated in her book Gender Outlaw, "I know I'm not a man -- about that much I'm very clear, and I've come to the conclusion that I'm probably not a woman, either."

I wasn't raised to be a man. I did not absorb male socialization. I did not have testosterone dominant in my body, with the resulting imperious sex drive, until I was 41 years old. I have never thought of women as other than my equal, and don't believe I can. I don't have any of the traditional attitudes considered male in this society. While I am capable of having a monotone discussion about sports, I'd rather have a passionate conversation about life.

I've become increasingly convinced, both through personal experience and through conversations with other trans people, that it's not really possible to transition fully from one sex to another. Biomen (men who were born male) see me as a man, though they quickly come to realize there's something not quite manlike about me. Many assume this must mean I'm gay (I don't identify as such), as the thought never enters their minds that perhaps I wasn't always male. Those biomen who know I'm trans sometimes utilize me as a resource for understanding women's ways of seeing the world, though I have always been treated respectfully by these men.

Biowomen see me as a man, though they quickly come to realize there's something not quite manlike about me. Women, however, tend to feel completely comfortable with me in a way many biomen do not -- they subconsciously recognize me as "one of them," though not in a way that makes me feel uncomfortable. It

126

does not feel as if they are seeing me as a woman. Rather, they seem to recognize me as a safety zone, a refuge from other men, of whom they feel they must be wary. I've had a number of biowomen comment with surprise on how comfortable they feel with me. Many of them, unaware that I'm trans, assume this must mean I'm gay. Because the mainstream view still equates "drag queen" and "transsexual," I've never met a bioman or biowoman yet who has figured out on their own that I was born female.

Now, I feel I'm neither man nor woman, though the limitations of English force me to choose sides, if only so I may have terminology with which to describe myself. So, I'm a guy, much more comfortable with male pronouns than female, but not really feeling like "a man." I'm living la vida medea -- life in the middle. I have not crossed the bridge from "female" on one side, over an immeasurable chasm, to become "male" on the other side. Rather, I have *become* the bridge.

To deny our own impulses is to deny the very thing that makes us human.                                        --Matt Doran, *The Matrix*

# ANDROGYNE:
# THE UNION OF OPPOSITES WITHIN
## Swadiksha Ananda*

*I hold a Medical Board license and national certification in massage therapy. I enjoy colonial American history, gardening, yoga, working out with stretch bands and running.*

I'm an androgyne person (pronounced an'-dro-gine, with a soft g). The Classical Greeks called persons who are both genders in the same body at the same time "Androgynes." Blessed with an existence that we cannot evade or conceal for very long without suffering psychological and emotional harm, we are, however, misunderstood in a society that enforces strict binary gender roles upon its members. This misunderstanding of our nature often places us under such strict social pressures that most of us make a sincere effort to exist in either one realm or the other. In other words, to be male or female. However androgynes cannot sustain this effort for very long without suffering harm.

Some of us are intersexed. Most of us are not. Not all of us are naturally androgynous looking. Not all androgynous looking people are androgynes. Transsexuals who undergo the transition process often reach a point in their transition in which they obtain an androgynous appearance. To them this is often at best something that needs to be tolerated in order to reach their goal of transitioning into the other gender. Many of them endorse the strict binary gender roles of society in general. This is to be expected as they experience a lifetime of pain seeking to move into their desired gender.

I was born a "male" and given the name of James. I grew up the middle child of three brothers. We lived out in the country where most of the neighborhood children were boys. In general my childhood was happy. We boys almost lived in the woods looking somewhat like children out of the pages of Lord of the Flies. I had a couple of female cousins my age. When they would visit they too

128

soon joined into our little tribe. So I never had a lot of opportunity to try to get involved much with girl's games or play. But in our play I often found myself more involved with the girls than the other boys. I soon realized as a child that I was not content to be only a boy. Since I was not, I found myself thinking I wanted to be a girl. At least girls were allowed to do boy things in addition to their own, even if they were called "tomboys." No one ever mentioned that it was O.K. to be both. In fact, it was made clear that boys do not do girl things.

One day I heard it mentioned that there was something called a "sex change." I was fascinated by the idea but did not dare let on how deep my interest ran. As I grew up, it became even more obvious to me that a sex change was the only hope of my finding freedom in such an un-free world.

My story as a perceived transsexual was not at all much different from that of most of the other true transsexuals in this book. I tended to overcompensate as a male to hide my hidden female needs. I was almost always tense, intense and depressed. I was blessed to find and to marry a woman who was very accepting of my true nature. Her acceptance was a key factor in my being able to find my true identity as androgyne. Eventually I connected with a doctor who prescribed female hormone therapy for me. As the physical changes occurred, I sought out even more of an androgynous wardrobe. I started to wear women's jeans and other clothing. They fit better. I was careful not to buy anything that would obviously be identified as women's. I also started to wear light subtle makeup. Our goal was to ease me into my new gender role.

My appearance soon became very androgynous for I, too, was in that in-between genders state that I mentioned previously. It was both paradise and a nightmare at the same time. About that time I legally changed my name from James to Jamie. I just seemed to drift into the female world while still maintaining my ties with the masculine. That happened in part because women could sense the changes in me and because I felt free to pursue my feminine side. I would have been happy to stay there except for two things. One was the pressure I felt being stared at while out in public. The typical "is that a man or a women?" That was never the case with people who knew me, though. The other was that I could not believe that it was possible to be what we called "bi-gender." My spouse believed that one could be, just as a person can be bisexual. I wanted to believe that, but I thought "I can't be the only one in the world like this." Nowhere did I read of androgyne. I never even heard the word. I recall typing in "androgynous" into search engines, looking for others and not finding any. So I decided to go full-time as a female. That was the other side of the gender coin.

I recall showing up as a woman at work. I still maintained certain aspects of an androgynous appearance. I never wore a dress, but restyled my hair and makeup and stopped wearing my sports bra that flattened me out. Everyone seemed to pretend not to notice. My situation was such that I was in a rather liberal work situation in a very blue collar town. Though they still referred to me with masculine pronouns at work, when I left the building I was called "ma'am" while out in public. I did not feel 100% comfortable in that role, either. I found myself overcompensating as a female in much the same manner I did as a male. For a long while I thought I just needed to relax and get used to it. Slowly I started to realize that I was a lot more happy when I was in that androgynous state. But I was faced with the dilemma of being a gender freak alone in the world.

Philosophers have wrestled for centuries as to why God allows many to suffer with birth defects and the like. It has taken the better part of a lifetime for me to realize that we androgynes hold a purpose on this earth. That purpose is to demonstrate that we are more than our bodies or our genders. We all are neither male or female in God's eyes. We are spirit.

I continue to remain on hormone therapy though I cut back some aspects of it. I dress androgynously. My hair is styled andro-gynously. My body has soft skin, minimal body hair and a female athletic type of physique. At times I'm considered to be male. Other times I'm thought to be female. Often times people have no clue as to where to place me. Yes, at times people are rude towards me but not as much as before. I'm much more able to forgive them now. I finally found others like me online. I feel comfortable in my skin and soul for the first time.

# PART VI

# TRANSGENDERED PEOPLE

# AS PARENTS

# ARE YOU GOING TO HAVE CHILDREN?
## Lydia A. Sausa

*I am currently an Adjunct Professor in the Human Sexuality Studies Program at San Francisco State University. I am, also, a professional Sexuality Educator, Trainer, and Consultant assisting schools and health service organizations to improve services for trans youth. Please contact me through the editor.*

"Are you going to have children?" I was asked at my first college LGBT Speakers Bureau event. I was one of the four student panelists featured that day in front of a large lecture hall of 200 students. I was doing so well. I had addressed and answered, to my own satisfaction, many personal questions that afternoon such as: "How did you know you were trans?" "Have you told your parents?" "How does your identity affect your religious beliefs?" "What types of people are you attracted to?" Our panel discussion was analogous to an exuberant tennis match, with provocative questions returned with sincere and illuminating replies. I was impressed with the panel speakers for being so honest and articulate, and proud of myself for participating since I had been out only a few months.

The bold student with black wire rim glasses in the front row once again asked the question that had initially caused me such amazement. "Are you going to have children?" The Q & A tennis match was over for me when this simple question hit me smack in the face. "Well, of course, why not?" I replied since it was a dream I have had since I was a child myself. The student then expanded on the original question, "have you thought of the problems your children are going to have because of who you are?" This 20-year-old student had not. That was the first day in my life in which I realized having children was not a given, a common life expectation, or a right that I possessed. That day I realized that having and raising children is a privilege.

This question of having and raising children has been

asked of me many times since that infamous day, often by curious friends, partners, and family members -- including my mother, a very traditional Roman Catholic woman who immigrated from a small rural town in Sicily. Most of the time my mother adores me, partly because I look a lot like my father who died suddenly when I was still in college, and partly because I inherited her quick wit and sense of humor. While we have a close relationship, there have been many days my mother and I have struggled because of her concerns about my safety, my gender-variant appearance, and employment opportunities, let alone having children and raising a family. She continually worries like many other mothers I know, caring for me and wanting the best for her child. It was not always easy for either of us as we learned about each other, our different wants, needs, and dreams; grieving those which could no longer exist, creating new ones as the years passed. I believe my mother needed to know that she did nothing wrong, and I needed to know I was and am a good kid. I love my mother and am grateful for all that she has given me, and only together could our relationship have matured and come so far.

What of my own children? As I am finally finishing up my Ph.D. (to my mother's incredulity) and looking forward to a career, I think about children constantly. I think about finding a caring, wise, and loving co-parent to raise them, I think about finding a safe place to live where they will not be harassed or discriminated against, I think about finding good schools and good people to share in their lives, and hoping they grow up feeling loved and appreciated. In essence, I worry like my mother does about me, because I, too, want the best for my children. Yet I must remember that children have their own lives to lead, and parents and caregivers can only do so much. We are mentors, guides, role models, and sometimes friends; regardless of what we do they will find their own unique paths as I did, and my mother before me when she immigrated to this country many years ago.

This morning I commented to my partner about the continually rising cost of a college education, concerned I will never be able to afford children, and was reminded of my mother's warnings that regardless of my multiple academic degrees, a career in education would be far from lucrative. My partner, who is an actor, turned to me and said jokingly that it will be cheaper if our children take after her and grow up to be artists. Ironic, isn't it, since my own mother has always fallen asleep during the plays I have taken her to see! I turned to my partner and said with a big smile, "Our children will be what they want to be and all we can do is love them."

\* \* \*

When my [CD then MtF] husband and I became adoptive parents of an autistic (severely emotionally disturbed) child who had lived at the residential school where I worked, most of the families in the school's parents' group could not understand why we would have taken on this "burden".... There was one couple, though, who told us, "You think you are doing this only for him, but *you will get much more back from your relationship with him than you ever give.*"

Thirty-two years later, we know the truth of what they said. Because of our autistic son, we went on to adopt seven more "special needs" children -- after the birth of our two homemade sons. Korean, Vietnamese, Chinese-American and African-American, the children came to us with challenges including cerebral palsy, post-polio, learning and language disabilities, and emotional/ behavioral difficulties due to their backgrounds. Their ages when they came to us ranged from three and one half to eighteen years old. Was it easy or always fun? No. It included hard work and frustration. There was also humor, and satisfaction, and love....

Although my husband's transgenderism is totally different from autism, my experience with it is in some ways similar, comprised of hurt and frustration and humor and love, and an overall sense of enrichment.

--Anne Giles, *Trans Forming Families*...

# BIRTHING NEW LIFE
## Loree Cook-Daniels

*I own WordBridges, a consulting firm specializing in conflict resolution and written communications. Marcelle, my partner of fifteen years, is a female-to-male transsexual, who transitioned after bearing our child. We live with our son, Kai, in Vallejo, California. Bio update: I am now a freelance researcher, writer and conflict resolution specialist based in Milwaukee, Wisconsin.*

It's one of the few regrets I have, that pregnancy.

It was a much-wanted pregnancy. It took fifteen months of trying, after more than a year and a half of negotiating, after seven years of fantasizing and mentally trying things on for size. And, of course, we'd never regret having the result of the pregnancy, our wonderful child, Kai. But the pregnancy itself was awful. Just thinking about it makes me tear up, four years after the fact.

\* \* \* \*

At first, I thought Marcelle was joking. After all, on the morning he woke me to say he'd decided to have our baby, the calendar said April 1st. But he wasn't fooling and, in fact, it was our best option. We believed my hormonal cycle too erratic to make insemination very feasible, and I had no desire to bear a child anyway. The adoption option seemed foreclosed. Every gay and lesbian family we spoke to who had successfully adopted told us that the only way it could be done was for everyone to pretend the relationship was just roommates. We didn't see how that would work for us, an interracial lesbian couple who had taken the in-your-face step of legally ensuring we had the same last name. Even the most denial-facile social worker and judge wouldn't be able to see their way around that particular signal that we were slightly more than roommates.

And, to be truthful, we thought the pregnancy might do

Marcelle good.   We had wanted a child so long that having Marcelle's hated female body produce such a miracle might, we thought, help him appreciate it more.

We were wrong.  Terribly wrong.

For nine months, Marcelle had trouble keeping a meal down.  He actually lost weight, although the baby found enough nourishment from existing stocks to come out, full-term, at nearly six pounds.  But it wasn't just the nausea, or even the scary bleeding, that was the problem.  It was that being pregnant, for Marcelle, was profoundly wrong.  He was not meant to endure those emotions, those inabilities, those...oh lord, most of all those...awful comments from others about how expectant mothers should act.

Suddenly thrust into the unfamiliar role of butch, I did my best to be supportive of this cranky, sick, depressed pregnant "wife."  But I was also struggling and angry.  After nine years of blocking Marcelle's transition, telling him he must choose either surgery or me, I had finally come to my senses.  The turning point had been two lines in a film we saw at the local lesbian and gay film festival.  A female-to-male transsexual said that he had had trouble coping with his transsexual feelings because he really didn't like men.  Then one day, he said, he realized that not all genetic men like men as a class, either.

It was my turning point, too.  Marcelle's misanthropy had always been one of my primary sticking points.  I couldn't imagine it was healthy to want to become something you clearly didn't like.  But our friend, Max, was right: men, as a class, in our society are not necessarily worth emulating.  But that doesn't mean one can't intend to, and be, a better sort of man.

Walking home from the film, I asked Marcelle if he still thought about transitioning.  His answer, given the years in which the topic had occupied our house unbroached, was stunning.

"Every day."

I took a few more silent, faltering steps, reeling with the implications of those two words.  How much pain I must have caused my lover and partner for all those years.

"Then I need to step out of your way," I finally, quietly, said.

Given that this conversation came after we had found a donor, negotiated all our legal agreements, and begun inseminating, my sudden change of heart meant revisiting some previous decisions. Marcelle decided he wanted to continue trying to get pregnant, and our donor said he had so little invested in gender that it didn't bother him any that one of the mothers of his child might well morph into another father to his child. So those potential barriers melted away.

But unexpectedly having that immovable obstacle called Loree cleared from his path turned out to confuse Marcelle. After two decades and more of dreaming of being male, he suddenly discovered that my opposition had completely overshadowed and hidden his own doubts, which now came out to bedevil us both. He couldn't, simply stated, decide for sure whether or not to transition.

Which made me nuts. Especially when we finally had a confirmed pregnancy, I needed to know: was my partner going to be male or female? Was my child going to have two mothers, or a mother and a father? Marcelle had to decide now, I frequently fumed aloud, because I didn't want my child to be confused by a parent's sex change. Marcelle would have to transition, I demanded, if he transitioned at all, shortly after the child's birth.

And so the pregnancy went. Marcelle coped badly, physically and emotionally. I veered crazily between trying to be supportive, feeling guilty over Marcelle's difficult pregnancy and my long opposition to his dream, and being angry that he could now not decide if he wanted to live that dream.

By the time Marcelle went into labor, we were already worn out. And we were completely unprepared for what finally emerged from his womb --a boy, after months of completely trusting the doctor's sonogram interpretation that we were expecting a girl!

"What did you say it was?" Marcelle reportedly asked the nurses each time he emerged from the anesthesia. "Did I dream you said it was a boy?" Yes, they assured him, it's a healthy boy. He kept nodding off again, reeling from the implications.

By the time we three left the hospital days later,

Marcelle had come to see Kai's unexpected gender as the universe's unmistakable signal. Kai was supposed to be a girl but turned out to be a boy, just like his Dad.

* *

Every birth creates at least three new lives. The child's life starts, of course, but his parents' lives alter, too, often so dramatically as to warrant a new designation.

In my case, Kai's birth made me not only a mother, but a wife. It made Marcelle not only a parent, but a man. Kai's birth changed our family from being a couple of out, activist Lesbian-feminists to a nuclear suburban family of Mommy, Daddy, and baby. Our beliefs and commitments are the same, but what we look like to others and the complex of expectations that comes with that perception, expectations that we must either fulfill or fight, have shifted dramatically. Treading our way through this unexpected and yet not unfamiliar (we grew up in it, after all) ocean of stereotypes about who Marcelle and I are as individuals and as a couple, particularly as we've been adapting to our roles as parents and learning who our new "roommate" is, has been challenging, to say the least. But it has also been invigorating and eye-opening, and we have learned and grown tremendously as a result. All of us are better people, we think, for having navigated these strange waters.

So, although I regret the pregnancy itself, I do not regret the lives it birthed. They were not the lives I expected, but then when do lives -- our own or others' -- turn out as expected? They are still good lives, filled with love and promise, wonder and mystery.

* *

Four years post pregnancy

I'm pleased to tell you we've won one! I was, today, granted my stepparent adoption of Kai, along with some groundbreaking "firsts." The judge had to, in essence, agree that Marcelle was legally male, that he and I are legally married, and that it's in Kai's best interest to have the law recognize his birth mother as his father and me as his mother. Our home-done insemination from a known donor also turned out to present some problems, but these, too, were resolved. Finally, Kai put in his

139

second-best life performance as a contrary. (The first was his birth, which was breach, having turned from head down just before delivery.) I'm told the judge smiled at his antics, probably figuring that if I was trying to adopt this kid, I was welcome to him!

Tonight I'm a very embarrassed, exhausted, but happy (and legal) mom!

UPDATE: Eight years post-pregnancy

It is with huge sadness that I report that Marcelle took his own life in the spring of 2000. Because we did secure that adoption, I was able to keep Kai and even obtain Social Security survivors' benefits for us (which other widows of FTMs have not been able to do). We have now formed a new family with Michael Munson, another FTM, to whom I literally owe my life. We are all now deeply engaged in learning the skills necessary to respond to and thrive with Kai's ADHD.

The day care teacher didn't know about our family history, but looking at the two of them, she had no doubt that Kai was Marcelle's child, "You couldn't deny that child if you wanted to," she told Marcelle one day. "He looks like you birthed him yourself."

Funny thing is, he did!

-- Loree Cook-Daniels

# TRANSPARENTING
## Lisa Lees

*I'm 50 years old, grew up in Missouri and Oklahoma, and have lived in Michigan since 1977. I've worked as a magazine editor, college teacher, technical writer, and systems analyst. For the past five years I have taught stage makeup for and helped run a nonprofit children's theater company in which both my children are involved.*

My daughter was five and my son was two and a half when I began to transition in 1994. Although there was some initial confusion with practical details such as pronoun and name, I don't see that there has been any lasting confusion or problems. We were open about the process and what was going on, so I suspect that our children simply saw this as another part of a complicated world. My spouse and I are still married, though we no longer have a romantic relationship. We continue to live together as the parents of our children.

I did not really discuss my transition with my children; they were too young to understand that grownups aren't generally allowed to make such changes. I answered their few questions and presented the process as something I needed to do. It's difficult for me to tell how much I changed as seen by other people. I don't feel that I changed very much (though people say I did), and perhaps I changed least in the eyes of my children, for my transition did not change my relationship with them or how much I was involved with their day to day care and upbringing.

I cannot recall any specific questions from my daughter. Whatever she did ask would have been answered with some variant of, "Because I want to / need to / feel that way." My daughter has always been a very "inner directed" kind of person who pays little attention to peer pressure or social norms, so I suspect that "because I want to" was a perfectly good answer for her. Other children might go on to wonder, "but what will ... think, or what will ... say about me."

As soon as I began to transition I became involved in LBGT activities on the campus where I worked. Both my children have been to many events, conferences and marches with me and have heard me speak to classes and seminars and workshops. Certainly this has affected them and made them aware of issues that many children may not hear about. They've also met and seen a wide variety of gender-variant people, and definitely understand that there are far more than two ways to be anything.

As usual I was buoyed by the thrill of finally transitioning and being able to speak about issues long held in the closet. It was my spouse who did most of the suffering, as her relationships and social position were turned topsy-turvy because she decided to remain married to me. There were times our family was shunned by homeschool groups, children invited to play who did not show up, and phone calls not returned as people decided that the easy way of dealing with our situation was to turn their backs on us.

My spouse's family is very conservative and do not approve of me (my beliefs, my politics, or that I am trans and queer). There was a strained period of a year or so following my transition when I saw something of my in-laws, but since then I have stepped out of the picture to reduce stress for all concerned. When my spouse takes our children to visit her parents, I cease to exist. (But my daughter calls me twice a day, so I'm not forgotten.)

My children (now ages 12 and 10) seem to be growing up with much less gender stereotyping than I see in most kids. This is probably due as much to their having always been home-schooled as to my talks about the social construction of gender. They are quite different from each other, and some of the ways in which they are different could be attributed to one being a girl and one a boy, but we don't do so.

My daughter does not have pierced ears, does not wear makeup off stage, sneers at the Toys'R'us distinction between girl toys and boy toys, subscribes to New Moon, reads science fiction by the ton, and likes violent video games. She'll scream if you drop a bug in her lap, then punch you out. She is in no hurry to grow up and is not looking forward to certain aspects of that process. Her

142

best, and only close, friend is the same-age daughter of a lesbian activist we got to know while I was working on campus.

My son is caring and sensitive, cries easily, rescues bugs (to his sister's chagrin), likes animals and flowers and trains and tall buildings (he was devastated by the events of 9/11). He bends over backwards to be nice to everyone. He has no close friends, but gets along easily with whoever he happens to be with, so long as they are nice to him. (I have noticed that his individuality is tolerated less by very young children, who often are not allowed to dress and look as they wish, than by older children beginning to make their own statements as individuals.)

My children play together constantly and are best friends, though they would not always admit it. They usually wear sweat clothes, but like costumes and pretending. When I look at them I see more first/second child differences than I do girl/boy differences. Often other people assume that they are both girls (usually) or boys because they don't do many of the typical things girls and boys do to assert a distinct gender identity (differences in hair, clothing, language, posture and so on).

One area of problems in transparenting is that of legal identity and relationship. I can prove who I am, but without explaining that I am transsexual and showing several pieces of paper which I do not usually carry with me, I cannot prove that I am married to my spouse or that I am a legal (not to mention biological) parent of my children. This impacts health care decisions, travel, and could be disastrous in an emergency. I feel very much that I am a second rate citizen in this country, whose rights have yet to be secured. Hence my activism and openness.

Perhaps my children will have some trouble "fitting in" as they go into the world as adults, but I don't see that as a negative thing. Those who hear the beat of a different drummer, who take the road less traveled, are often the people who shape the future. I hope, with some confidence, that my children will be among those who shape the more tolerant and understanding world that we so urgently need.

# FROM THE MOUTHS OF BABES: THE TRUTH
## C. Daniel Winkenhofer

*I am a 40 year old FTM, who came into fatherhood approximately three years ago. My SO and I "met" in a lesbian chatroom; I told her about myself even before we met in person. I have been employed as a social worker/therapist for 17 years and am active in several transgender organizations. I come from a well-educated family who have accepted my transition.*

From day one of my first in-person meeting with Melissa, her son came into the room and just said hi. He was four at the time; her daughter was even younger. He accepted me and I was just a guy to him. We didn't know how or when to tell him about me, nor his father, who lives in another state. Approximately two years ago Melissa and the children moved in with me. Luckily, their bio dad had no problems with this.

First I was Danny, then suddenly Daddy Danny. No prompting; the kids came up with that on their own. Even though I had not started transitioning yet, they still knew. Somehow, someway children always know. Our youngest daughter who will soon be four used to cry and push me away, but for a long time now, it's not been that way. If I ask her to do something it's, "But Daddy..." Or "Daddy, you're so handsome...," "before you go to work, would you...?"

One night we heard our then six year-old son telling his dad on the phone, "Grandma Nancy (my mom) is confused, sometimes she thinks Daddy Danny is a girl." When our daughter goes to my endocrinologist appointments with me, she watches Daddy Danny get shots. Our son just asks me if it hurts; he knows that this helps me grow a mustache. He also comes to me a lot and tells me he is growing one, also, or getting hair on his back now.

On another occasion, another young three year-old girl visited with her two moms, both lesbians. This child said to

Samantha I was a mommy, but Sam said, "No, that's my daddy," and made a fist. Our seven year-old was also heard telling a friend that I was a boy, period. This child had not known me by anything other than given name, but our son enlightened him.

Around that time, I told our seven year-old that sometimes people are just born with the wrong parts, that I really was a boy inside, but had to take medicine and have operations to make me look more like a boy. We made this very simple for him and he seemed to understand. When we go out the children call me Daddy always, no exceptions. At first I was taken aback, not used to it; now I embrace it, even if I do get a look now and then. I also insisted to my mom, even though I knew it would take her awhile, to never refer to me as a girl in front of the kids and she hasn't. She just had never thought about it before. Melissa's mom read some Internet links I sent her, has never ever called me anything but Dan, and thanked me for caring for her daughter and grandchildren.

When I dress my daughter, talk to my son about sports, etc., I feel this completeness. I did not need to give birth to these children to make them mine.

We have had ups and downs but the biggest down had nothing to do with transition; just moving was hard on our son and he missed his bio dad. Teachers, health providers, etc., never say anything to me. I just say I am the other parent. Melissa and I attend conferences and school functions together as parents.

We have never specifically told the children's biological father, but we get along and feel he would be OK with this. Matter of fact, the last two times I have been around him he called me Danny; yesterday on the phone he told the children, "Be good for Mommy and Danny." In my heart I am certain our children did the education. All they ever want is to be loved, cared for and safe. Our kids just happen to have two dads and lots of grandparents and cousins and such.

My advice would be to give people time, keep it simple with children and be honest if they ask questions. That has helped us become a complete and accepted family to everyone we know. We are very, very fortunate and I am immensely proud to be a dad.

# CHILDREN
## Robyn Walters

*I have four daughters and six granddaughters. Adding my husband's family brings our totals to eight children and 13 grandchildren. I'm a semiretired naval engineer, author of articles and short stories, member of PFLAG and several transgender support and advocacy organizations, and a spiritual healer. Life is full, and I am free.*

I don't know why some children stay and some children run. I suppose there are many families who can say the same thing. The lure of the fast life? The yen for greater things? Shame about parent's education, social standing, lack of wealth? Embarrassment over a parent's life changes?

Sitting at the dinner table one summer evening while our daughters were home from college, my wife had a banshee wailing session. The kids, the two youngest of my four daughters, gave us the what-is-going-on look. Despite our decision not to reveal to the girls what I had told my wife a week earlier, she blurted out, "Are you going to tell them, or shall I?"

"Um, well, girls, I am a crossdresser. I like to wear women's clothes." "Oh, thank goodness," said our older daughter. "Is that all? I thought you were maybe a pedophile or something, what with the young models in those Victoria's Secret catalogs."

"I knew that," said my youngest daughter. It was her last comment for several years. From that moment on, she has avoided me. She never mentioned the subject until her mother and I divorced and I had married again. It is as if I have ceased to exist for her. Two of my daughters are accepting, and two have run.

In the five years since I moved west, I've seen my youngest daughter only once. It was more than three years ago at the funeral of my granddaughter, my second daughter's youngest child. Even though I was making my last-ever appearance in male-mode, my youngest managed to avoid me and left without introducing her boyfriend or saying good-bye.

During the same five years, I've seen my two oldest daughters a few times and my third daughter dozens of times. I see her every time I go east for work. She was even in the wedding party when my husband and I married, two years ago.

Yes, my husband. I was wrong about being a crossdresser back when I was 58. Once I accepted the long-repressed fact of being transgendered, my personal transition accelerated. I was wheeled out of surgery on my 63rd birthday, a new woman. I awoke to see my husband coming into the room. A year later, I watched as he was brought back from surgery, a new man.

My two youngest daughters were born less than two years apart. Both were brought up the same, with lots of loving support. Why is one supportive and okay with her father being female and the other, not? I wish I knew. If I did, then there might be something I could do other than to send birthday presents, Christmas presents, and the occasional email. If I knew, perhaps I could take some positive action to win her back.

But I don't know. I suspect that it has more to do with who they are than with who I've become. If beauty is in the eye of the beholder, then so too are other impressions and judgments. I know that what others may think of me is none of my business, but I cannot help but wonder if there isn't some piece of information that might give my youngest an 'aha' moment and make her value the love she has thrown away. But I don't know.

What I do know is that transsexuals don't wake up one morning and decide over breakfast coffee to change sex. "Oh, what a beautiful day. I think I'll turn our family life upside down. Oh, I know; I'll become a girl." No, it doesn't work that way. Instead, we struggle to conform to what family and society expect of us. We avoid hurting others while our own internal hurt, confusion, guilt, and disappointment grow to an overwhelming pressure over the years. Change or die.

What else do I know? I know that I am not selfish. I am being true to who I am.

I know I'm happy that two of my four daughters gladly accept me in their lives. I'm not Mom, but I am fully female and fully Dad to them, and it is a wonderful feeling of belonging. I know that I am not happy to have lost some whom I love. I loved my wife, but she loved an image, not the person. I love all my children, but two reject me, and it hurts.

Nor am I happy that some in society consider me and my transsexual brothers and sisters to be the devil's spawn. It isn't easy to be reviled, but I sometimes have to chuckle about that. What those people don't know is that I have accepted the transsexual birth defect challenge God gave me, and I have grown in grace and wisdom. I am whole. I am happy with myself. And I know that God is happy with the strength I have shown in overcoming the challenge of my transition.

For, you see, I am a child, too. I am a beloved child of God, as are the children of my flesh. I cannot be angry with the youngest child who rejects me, for she knows not what she does. The same holds true for my oldest daughter, who began avoiding me after several years of saying she was my most tolerant child. As we all grow in wisdom and grace, I pray that one day we shall be close again.

"Big deal, Dad," they'll say. "One little thing."

The experience of dealing with any special circumstance has the potential for difficulties, but also possibillity for many positive results. The two Chinese characters for crisis mean danger and opportunity.                    -- Ann Giles

***

I'm an MTF mother of an eighteen month old daughter. She was conceived with my sperm, frozen before my transition. I tell people I'm her sperm mother!                    --Helen Reed

148

# THE FUTURE CAN BE CONTROLLED
## Lisa Miller

*I traveled around the world at age ten, but lived my teen years in the Washington, DC area. I earned a degree in chemical engineering and spent 25 years working on fascinating projects for three major corporations. I got a pilot's license, and held an elected political office. Then, two years ago, my real education began.*

For years our family has been an island of stability in a world with no rules. We have endured as we have watched close friends divorce, children turn to drugs or crime, families suffer frustration and death and psychoanalysis. Our circle of acquaintances includes more than one family where all members are taking Prozac or Paxil or Zoloft, even the pets. As the years have passed, the three of us have been proud of our commitment to each other; Marylee and I married 23 years ago, and our daughter Andrea is now 20.

The summer of 2000 put our stability to the test: I finally worked up the courage to reveal my true self to Marylee. I am a transsexual, although at the time that I told her, I had great difficulty explaining the meaning of this. To my relief, she understood that I was born this way, rather than making a choice and excluding her. Our concerns initially revolved around deep and basic questions: "How can we continue to have a relationship?" "what does the future hold for us?" "what do we tell people?" We also anguished about the effect on our daughter of having her father, her male role-model, transition before her eyes. The timing of my coming out was partly calendar-based; Andrea was due to start college in August 2000, and I felt that having her out of the house would give us time to plan carefully before we revealed our secret to her.

We decided not to tell Andrea until Spring 2001. We had planned a trip to see my father and explain everything to him, and we felt that would also be a good time to tell Andrea. Visits to

Andrea at college in October and November were straightforward; it was cold enough in Vermont for me to wear bulky clothing which hid my changing physique. My earrings (a big departure from my past conservative lifestyle!) I explained away as a response to mid-life crisis -- actually quite close to the facts. I also found that my personality had really not changed much, even though the hormones had altered my ways of thinking; I still presented to Andrea the father that she had always known.

As Christmas 2000 approached, Andrea came home on semester break. Marylee and I both looked forward to this time together, and we had discussed some specific do's and don'ts for us to follow while Andrea was home. These involved being careful to not talk about therapy, shopping, the support group, or anything else connected to my new life. For two weeks everything went smoothly, although I was on edge most of the time due to being so premeditated in everything I said. In retrospect, I'm sure Andrea was puzzled by a vague peculiarity in my actions, but she said nothing and neither did we.

On Christmas Eve, it happened. My father, 74 at the time, was visiting us for the holidays. We had gotten a new computer, and Andrea was using it. I was not proficient in using the new machine, and I did not hide my "Lisa Tries Out the World" website well enough to avoid discovery by Andrea. She found it, viewed it, and then came down the stairs in a daze and said "Mom, I think you'd better come here." She cried, and I felt horrible for her, for her shock and for her feeling of betrayal. The rest of that day was the most peculiar of our lives. Marylee explained my situation to Andrea, and also explained that my father did not yet know and we were not ready to tell him. That night, the three of us talked while my father was watching TV, and I think Andrea's initial fears of our family disintegrating were soothed, but she was still very much in shock and completely at a loss for words.

A few days later, my father departed and we had time to discuss things in depth. Andrea was still baffled by my trans-sexualism; I apparently had done a good job over the years of being a true father and it was very poignant to see her have to give up her idealized view of me. The hurt in all of us was deep, and there was nothing that could displace it. Early in January 2001, I had an appointment with my therapist, and Andrea saw me as Lisa for the first time. She was amused, scared, and confused all at the same time. During her stay at home, her outward demeanor spoke of acceptance, but inwardly she was going through the stages of grief that we all know so well -- her anger had faded, but she was very much in denial about 'losing' her father. She returned to college in mid-January, and Marylee and I reverted to our long-distance relationship with her.

Andrea suffered more than we realized from this disruption to her life. Her next semester at college was an academic disaster; her ability to focus on schoolwork was minimal. She returned home for the summer of 2001 with a feeling of dread, worried about being allowed to return to college and worrying about being confronted with her non-father all summer. The three of us visited my therapist twice, which may have been a slight help to her in hearing transsexualism discussed in a matter-of-fact, nonjudgmental way. Andrea gradually admitted that my situation had occupied a lot of her thinking during school, and distracted her very much. She had never been totally open to us (all three of us can be somewhat stoic), and reaching true acceptance required all of us to be very open. This is a difficult adjustment, to change the way we relate to each other, but it slowly started to happen. Andrea at one point stated that "after this, I feel like I can tell you anything." But still, she was going through the depression stage of grieving, and we were powerless in altering its course.

Meanwhile, Marylee and I had reached some middle ground in our struggle to redefine our lives. We spoke openly about our fears, we found new common interests, and we stopped trying to predict the future. Our relationship had changed somewhat, but it was still based on love and mutual respect. I drew strength from Marylee's ability to ignore society's pressures and to think for herself. I began to see her true strength of character, and admired her for it; many of these are her attributes that I should have seen all along, but never did. It took an upheaval of my own world to be able to see how beautiful a person Marylee is.

Andrea's next semester at college was no better than the previous one; she returned home for Christmas 2001 hanging by an academic thread. We spoke bluntly and at length about her goals, her desires in life, and about the realities she faced. She needed to put aside her thoughts about me and concentrate on her own life. I think Andrea this time took the message to heart. Our holidays were marked by calm and love, in stark contrast to the previous Christmas. She was starting to emerge from the depression phase of grieving, as she saw in Marylee and me our continuing commitment to each other, our love, and a continuation of the parental support that was and is important to her.

Early this year, during a phone call with Andrea back at college, she remarked offhandedly that "she may never understand this, but she can accept it". She was speaking of the new me, and those words were sweet indeed. If I had to lose my daughter or my wife to be my true self, I would have a hollow existence and a sad one. That simple statement from her spoke volumes about her adjustment, and not coincidentally, her academic performance this past semester has been wonderful. It appears that Andrea has reached the acceptance stage of the grieving process, never willing to give up her image of what a father should be, but able to adapt to the present. She is home for a short time this summer, and our family life has returned to the humor, the fun, and the comfort that it formerly had.

We have survived a powerful and primal blow to our family, and have grown stronger from it. How did we do it? It took time. It took trust. It took love. And more than anything, we didn't give up on each other. Our future will never be as easy as it is for straight families, but ours might be much more interesting. And we're happy!

\*\*\*

Life is short and we have never too much time for gladdening the hearts of those who travel with us. Oh, be swift to love, make haste to be kind.                     --Henri Amiel
(Rev. Audette Fulbright)

# NURTURING MY GRANDCHILD
## Roxie Lynn Howard

*I am a post-op transsexual who has been a parent, a single parent, a grandparent and a foster parent. I enjoy photography and travel, and have not been employed outside the home in several years. My husband, Tom, is a retired History professor. In this story I have changed all names, except my own and my husband's.*

My daughter, Kathy, was having serious mental health problems. Her husband, Steve, had been removed from their home by Protective Services after my daughter had arrived home and found him naked with my four-year-old granddaughter, Jill. They suspected he had sexually abused Jill. While Steve admitted in writing to masturbating in front of Jill, he denied sexually abusing her. My grandchildren were in Foster Care. It was all overwhelming, and this was only the beginning!

My home was a place where the grandchildren felt safe and comfortable, and they had found refuge there in the past. After Social Services became involved, I continued to try to help. At the outset, I disclosed to Social Services that, while my daughter called me "Mom," I was also her genetic father. In order to help the social worker better understand transsexual issues, I gave her an article on gender and sex that my husband, Tom, and I had written. It was scary to disclose this in North Dakota, a state without a human rights commission and no legal rights or protections for transsexuals.

We were told Social Services had no real provisions for grandparents' visits I could share my daughter's visits with the grandchildren if she wished. I found it strange to be visiting Jill and her two-year-old brother, Keith, at Social Services in a room with a two-way mirror. Social Services came to consider me a positive influence on both my daughter and her children.

The children remained in the first foster home for only

about thirty days, because the foster mother felt she could not give Jill the special attention she felt Jill would need. Jill was acting out while getting dressed, making sure her socks were perfectly straight and getting very upset if they were not. I sensed she was simply trying to control something in her chaotic life.

When the children moved into their second foster home, Social Services decided that they would spend every other weekend in my home and that visitations for all family members would take place there. During the first two visitations I noticed my grand-children were becoming more withdrawn. Was it a normal adjust-ment to Foster Care, or were there other problems? I did know that the foster parents had started asking me to come to the back door when I called for the children. I phoned the foster home, as did my ex-spouse, Katie, who was also visiting the children in my home. The foster parents presented many problems. I also was intently aware of feeling the foster parents' personal prejudice toward me.

On Monday the telephone lines between family members and Social Services were a flurry of activity. They investigated, held a meeting, and promptly moved the children the following evening. I had never seen a bureaucracy move so quickly! We were assured the third foster home was competent with a record of success.

The third foster mother also had problems with Jill, which, within two and one-half months, reached a serious stage. On a non-visitation weekend the foster mother called me to explain how she was unable to handle Jill's issues.

At the subsequent meeting Foster Care offered two options concerning Jill. The first was to place her in our home. The other was to place her in a PATH home. A PATH home is for children with serious mental health problems. We agreed to take Jill into our home. We were told to enroll her in Head Start rather than kindergarten because of her emotional problems. It was also decided to leave Jill's brother, Keith, in his current foster home because he was doing well.

We placed Jill in a preschool half days. The director of the preschool told Foster Care two months later that she felt Jill could begin kindergarten. Foster Care agreed. My granddaughter began to blossom and grow in our home. She began to address her fears. Her obsession with her clothes soon disappeared. It was clear to me that it was not an obsessive-compulsive behavior but Jill's way of controlling something in her out-of-control world. Jill and I had a bond. This bond was clearly an asset.

One evening in the bathroom as I reminded Jill to wash her private parts, and to remember that no one but a doctor or nurse touches her private parts, Jill suddenly said, "My daddy did." I asked if she was getting a bath when he did that. She told me no and went on to describe the same setting and conditions the day my daughter walked in and found Steve naked with Jill. Steve was never charged with sexual abuse. Sadly, I was also informed that masturbating in front of your four-year-old daughter is not illegal in North Dakota. Even children lack some protections in North Dakota.

Jill's therapist came to a Foster Care meeting about five months after we had Jill and said, "I cannot give this girl a diagnosis. She is doing too well." Jill continued to bloom more with each passing day. Eventually it became clear that the children's mother, due to her illness, would never be able make a home for them. Both parents agreed to termination of their parental rights.

Jill was placed with her new adoptive parents December 22nd. The Foster Care worker sent us a lovely thank you note. Foster care considered this a wonderful success story. Jill's recovery was unbelievable. The foster parents from the third foster home adopted Keith. Tom and I still see both grandchildren and they still see each other. My ex-spouse, Katie, died of breast cancer 34 days after Jill was placed with her new parents.

Following Katie's death our 16-year-old son, who had been living with his mother, went to live with her sister. Katie and I had planned this years before in case her cancer became terminal. Unfortunately, neither he nor Katie's sister had ever accepted my transition. It very quickly became clear that for me to attempt co-parenting with that family would not be healthy for my son, so I reluctantly consented to their adopting him.

What a strange twist of fate to have succeeded so well in Foster Care with my grandchildren only to lose my own son a few months later!

# NATURE LOVES A CONTINUUM

One important thing we have learned from our trans-gendered friends is that nature loves a continuum. Just as we are not limited to tall and short, smart or stupid, even gay or straight, so, also, there is a gender spectrum. Some men are macho or gentle; women, too. Some are more in the middle and some, who find they were born in the wrong body or have elements of both genders, can now make the necessary bodily changes to present themselves as they truly are, inside.

We must realize it took this country a couple hundred years to accept gradations of skin color. Until the middle of the 20th century, if you were 1/16 black, you were black. Mulatos were not acknowledged and all but white folks suffered -- still do -- heavy discrimination.

More recently, both the straight and gay communities have been leery of bisexuals. They have wondered if people self-identify as bi simply from fear of coming out as gays. To refuse to see people for what they sincerely insist they are is like ignoring the child who raises his hand day after day in class and is never called on, never acknowledged. It is a kind of silent, but killing violence.

Let us learn from our history and more quickly come to understand and accept all types of transgendred people. Can you imagine a world where we have all learned just one simple thing -- to accept others as they are!

* * *

Benjamin Franklin is reported to have said that all of mankind is divided into three classes: Those who are immovable, those who are movable, and those who move. I say: Let us be the movers and focus on those who are movable. --Both, Mary Boenke

# PART VII

## THERAPISTS' COMMENTS

# IN THE BEST INTEREST OF THE CHILD
## Barbara F. Anderson

*I am in San Francisco and write for many TG newsletters as well as TGforum. My work time is split between a private practice and coordinating a program for the city of San Francisco called Gender Identity Treatment Services. I live with my husband, have three grown children and in my spare time enjoy hiking, gardening, and mysteries.*

One of the most challenging issues brought to a therapist is that of disclosing and explaining transgender behavior to children in a family. This article will focus on helping parents keep the best interests of their children predominant as they contemplate disclosure of a transgender parent.

Patty and Paul came to me to resolve a disagreement over whether to tell their teenage son, Pete, about Paul's crossdressing. Pete had found female clothing in Patty's closet that he knew was not his mother's. He confronted his parents separately and was clumsily put off by each until they could seek professional advice. While Patty had known of and accepted Paul's dressing for years, she had never planned to reveal this to their son. Paul felt that this was as good a time as any to tell him.

After eliciting a description of Pete's psychological adjustment (stable), and his relationship with his parents (good), a new question arose. Why was Pete rummaging through his mother's closet? It occurred to all three of us that Pete, himself, might be a crossdresser. It was decided that these parents should reveal to Pete his father's proclivity, in view of the possibility that the boy was similarly inclined and needed support and information about this behavior. Should it develop that there is another explanation for Pete's interest in his mother's closet, his stable psychological adjustment, good relationship with his parents, and their acceptance of cross-dressing in their home, would predispose Pete to accept his father's behavior with a minimum of discomfort.

This is an example in which two parents were able to put their child's needs first and make secondary their concerns about Pete telling a friend, losing respect for his parents, or any one of a number of less important issues.

Lila and Lester were the parents of three sons. They had a relationship of conditional affection and respect. In other words, Lila's affection and respect was conditional on Lester's keeping his crossdressing under wraps. That meant he was strictly limited with regard to when and where he could dress. Under no condition was he to socialize with other CDs or leave the house dressed. The consequences could be that his crossdressing behavior would be revealed to their sons.

They came to therapy because Lester was increasingly interested in meeting and socializing with other transvestites ever since a chapter of a national "sorority" was established in a nearby town. Lila saw this interest as an escalation of his "problem" which could only be contained by threats of the harshest measures. It was clear to me that she meant business as she explained that if she "lost" Lester, she had no intention of sharing their children with him.

Lila is a good example of a woman so obsessed with controlling her spouse's behavior that she had lost sight of her children's best interests. It was only when I asked her how she would feel if her children blamed her for telling on their father and instead, rallied around him and deserted her, that she reconsidered her position. This bought time to work with her around developing an understanding and appreciation of each parent's role in the lives of their children.

Neither parent has the right to deprive a child of a loving and competent parent, even if that parent has characteristics, ideas or values that conflict with those of the other parent. Infantile parents with unresolved dependency needs are the ones who have the most difficulty subsuming their needs in the interest of those of their children. Not only are they causing their children psychic pain, they are creating a new generation of parents who may, in turn, exploit their own children.

Counseling can reverse that pattern by providing

parents with a model of responsible behavior, and children with parents who are invested in their children's best interests.

Perhaps the most important [basic truth of mankind], typically honored more in the breach than the observance, is the truism enshrined in the Shakespearean admonition, "To thine own self be true." The path of integrity and self-discovery, however risky, can lift the human spirit to new levels of spontaneity, sensitivity and creativity. For anyone to realize their highest potential--be they straight, gay or trans; black, white, yellow or brown -- they need first to be able to utter the simple words, "I am what I am, and that's OK" .....

Foremost among [our social] standards, these crimpers of the soul, are our stereotypical gender roles. Little boys shouldn't cry or show emotion. Little girls should be demure and passive. How many millions of personalities have been warped, and lives thereby ruined, by even these most simple of everyday strictures?

Imagine, then, the courage inherent in defying not merely the notion of gender roles, but the traditional concept of gender itself!

-- Robert Bernstein, author of
*Straight Parents/Gay Children*

161

# BOY + FEMININE = TRAUMA
## Catherine Tuerk, M.A., R.N., C.S.

*I am a nurse psychotherapist in private practice in the metro Washington, DC area, specializing in GLBT issues , and recently received a grant to expand outreach to parents of gender variant children. I am married to Jonathan Tuerk, a psychiatrist, also in private practice. We have a straight daughter and a gay son. I am the immediate past president of the Metro DC chapter of PFLAG. For information on the groups discussed below, contact the editor.*

Thirty-three years ago I gave birth to a very gentle boy, who spent his early years having his feminine interests thwarted by parents who were instructed by mental health professionals to police his cross-gender interests in order to insure that he would not become gay. We dutifully and misguidedly subjected our son to soccer, which he hated, karate to teach him how to fight, and four years of psychoanalysis. Subsequently, we regretted the path we had taken, even though we did it as a result of "professional" advice. As a result, I made a commitment to do everything possible to prevent this abuse by parents of their own gender-variant children.

Three years ago, Edgardo Menvielle, a child psychiatrist, and I decided to start a support group for parents of young gender variant children, meaning those whose preferred clothing, toys, and play are often deemed unusual for their gender. Our advertisement in The Washington Post reads, "A Positive Parenting Support Group for Parents of Very Gentle Boys and Tomboy Girls. Meets monthly."

When parents pick up the telephone and inquire about the group, this is the last thing that they ever thought they'd have to do. They are afraid that their children will be gay or something worse. They instinc-tively feel that if they could inhibit their children's cross-gender behaviors, somehow that would change their fate. They come reluctantly -- for guidance and support from other parents, and because they are as isolated and as distressed as their children are. Everything that they need to do may seem counter-intuitive. Over time, they come to accept the fact that it is likely their child may grow up to be a sexual minority and that they did not cause it nor can they change it.

A fifteen-year longitudinal study done by Richard Green and documented in his book, *The Sissy Boy Syndrome*, indicated that 80% of gender variant boys are gay, transgendered or some sexual minority. Since that classic study, which was completed in the 1980s, many feel that the percentage may even be higher. At the end of the study, out of the 66 boys studied, only one identified as transgendered.

Most of the inquiries about our group come from the parents of boys. This is consistent with other settings, in which there are ten inquiries concerning boys for every one concerning a girl. This ratio probably exists because society tolerates and even rewards tomboy behaviors in girls, while it castigates feminine behaviors in boys.

In our group of eight parents, all are parents of boys, ranging in age from three to fourteen years. Each gender variant child is different, but all the children in our group have strong and persistent interest in opposite gender toys, play or clothing. They all, very typically, are extremely interested in Barbie dolls.

Generally speaking, as gender variant children mature (around the age of nine or third grade), they become increasingly aware of social stigma. Their cross-gender interests tend to go underground and become confined to private play and fantasy. As with all children, their interests mature and their repertoires expand. We do not know what the normal development of these children would be because they are always subjected to cultural stigma. (Children who express strong and persistent inter ests and behaviors that do not fit the stereotypic norms of masculine and feminine can be labeled in a variety of ways – "gender non-conforming," "cross-gender," "gender atypical" or "gender variant." We use the term "gender variant" because we want to encourage a positive attitude toward diversity.)

## PARENTS AND THE GROUP

Our group has come to realize that parents often need to grieve over the anticipated loss of the child they expected to have. Even though the child's sexual or gender identity is not clear in the early years, both the child and the parents know the child is different. Because the out-come is uncertain, it is sometimes hard for parents to resolve their grieving and move on. Most children begin the process of defining that "difference" or arrive at a definite conclusion about their sexual identity around puberty. Perhaps because gender identity is a socially outspoken concept, some children are sure they are "other" from as early as two or three years old. Parents need to be aware of their child's struggle and help in any way they can. Sometimes that means simply waiting for the child to "come out" or self-identify.

To help parents with the grieving process, we examine negative stereotypes of gay and transgendered people. We also explore the positive aspects of these people's lives, including having children. And we talk about the advances in medicine that allow trans people the treatment and respect they need to become whole. Sometimes gay and trans people visit the group and share their stories. We also provide educational books and videos. One of our parents attended the True Spirit Transgender Conference and shared her enlightening and positive experiences.

## THE PARENTS' JOB

The mantra of our group is "help your kid feel good and fit in." We try to show our parents how they can develop their children's self-esteem and appreciate their unique gifts. The parents also need to learn how to help their children negotiate a culture into which they do not fit easily and which may not readily accept them.

First, they must create a safe home environment where the child is free to express his interests and feelings without fear or shame. For instance, perhaps a boy child can wear dresses or make-up, at least sometimes, at home. Every child needs to feel loved unconditionally for who he or she really is. His special talents need to be affirmed. Even young children try to cope with all the disapproval that they sense in the outside world. They start

164

to feel that they are bad, that they are weak, that they are girls or half-girls or something so confusing that they have to escape into fantasy where they can be whole and fine. Parents need to empathize with the child's distress and must help clarify these issues as best they can. They might tell the child, "Sometimes boys like girl things and sometimes boys feel like girls and that's O.K." or "When you grow up you will find other people who are like you," or "We will help you be the kind of grownup person that you want to be."

Next, the parents have to help the children fit into the larger community as best they can. Like parents of other minorities, parents of gender variant children need to help their children realize that some people in the world can't understand or tolerate differences. They can be cruel or say unkind things. They may have to make some compromises in order to be comfortable outside the home. For example, a boy who wants to wear a fancy silk cape to school may be convinced to carry a square of the silk in his pocket instead. In order to make such compromises tolerable, the parents have to be constantly supportive and empathetic, helping the child understand that they (the parents) know how hard this is for the child.

Frequently, gender variant children feel lonely and isolated. Parents need to try to find creative outlets that are gender neutral and should never force children into hyper-masculine or hyper-feminine activities. Parents can help their children find supportive friends and they can tell children, "It's hard to feel lonely, but lots of people feel lonely a lot of the time. It's O.K. and you are O.K. Someday you will probably meet other people who are a lot like you and you will probably feel a lot happier."

### THE BENEFITS OF MEETINGS OTHERS
There are no easy answers for the problems encountered by gender variant children and their parents. However, talking about the problems with others seems to help. Sharing strategies, sharing feelings and fears, knowing about or meeting other children like theirs encourages the parents to be constantly affirming of the children. Ideally, the children need a chance to

meet each other, which can be an almost miraculous kind of affirmation for them. Finding out that you are not the only "different" boy in the world engenders a very special feeling.

After our group's first yearly family social outing, one father who had been very reluctant to attend the event, stated, with tears in his eyes, that this was the first time he had ever seen his son be socially comfortable.

A few of the children now have their own support group with Dr. Menvielle. Our hope for the future is to have a group for parents of girls, and to keep working until support groups for gender variant children are as common as any other family support groups in today's challenging and changing world. In lieu of such a group, we certainly encourage parents to read, to talk by phone or email with other parents, and to seek others with whom they and their children can identify so they can share their concerns, their pride and joys in their special, fascinating children.

Never doubt that a small group of committed persons can change the world. As a matter of fact, it is the only thing that ever has.                        -- Margaret Mead

(Arnold M. Drake & others)

# ISSUES FOR TRANSGENDERS IN THERAPY
## Martha Harris, MSW, LCSW

*After earning my social work degree in 1989, I founded the Banyan Counseling Center, Inc. in Alexandria, Virginia, seven years ago. My work has focused on the transsexual com-munity and I do regular outreach to educate the community about the issues many transsexuals face.*

I knew that opening my own counseling center would be a challenge because of the great number of therapists in the Washington, DC metropolitan area. For a few years, another therapist in this area had been talking to me about his work with transgender clients, mentoring me all those years, telling me how he handled the various tasks in helping someone through a transition process. I decided to let myself become known to that community as an understanding therapist who cared about their life changes, and did not consider it a psychiatric issue but rather a condition of birth which needed to be changed in order to feel right. There just weren't enough therapists who understood gender that way.

My clients and I cover many issues during our time together. Each client's story is unique, yet there are issues which many clients share. Of course, often the main reason someone seeks out the help of a therapist is for referrals -- one, for hormones and, two, a letter from me (and/or a letter from a psychologist or psychiatrist) for sex reassignment surgery (SRS). My clients are told that I can be more than JUST a referral for them. Working together, they can learn to become a woman or man and adjust to society's beliefs about their decision. It just so happens that 90% of my trans clients are male-to-female; only 10% are female-to-male. I currently do not have any clients who are crossdressers or are intersex. Our society seems to accept more easily female-born people who want to become male than male-born people who want to become female. Since, it is easier for a female-born person to live as a male than the other way around they do not seek a therapist's help in as great a number.

Almost universally, my clients arrive with an urgency to start hormones. Due to the accessibility of hormones through the Internet, there is more opportunity to start hormones before seeking the referral of a therapist to an endocrinologist. That causes a dilemma for therapists today. The usual three-month evaluation period is often curtailed due to the client's felt need for an immediate referral to an endocrinologist. In any event, when hormones are started, my clients feel a deeper level of inner peace. Hormones are powerful, but they do not usually take effect immediately. There can be an initial euphoric feeling because taking that hormone represents finally taking care of oneself. There can be a powerful emotional connection and a sense of coming home -- finally being right with the world. This emotional sense of well-being may actually help strengthen the transsexual during the period of coming out to loved ones.

The topic of how to tell spouses, partners, parents, siblings, and children is often of major concern to my clients. After assessing the history of their relationships, we develop a plan of how to tell loved ones. Above all, it is important that there be no secrets within close family relationships. As the body experiences physiological changes, how, in fact, is one to hide them? If the family has not seen the transgendered person for some time, they will probably see a marked difference and will wonder what has happened. Eventually, family members will figure it all out and they may resent the fact that they were not trusted earlier with the information. Even though there may be a period of rejection by parents, I have found that, if the relationship was healthy before transition, it will survive this major change in the relationship structure.

I have suggested a number of strategies to use in telling loved ones. Mothers, I have found, tend to feel blame for their child's gender identity problem because of something they might have done during pregnancy --even though they cannot figure out what that might have been. It is important to let mothers know that they are not to blame. It is more likely that some unusual biochemical event occurred during pregnancy, but that probably had nothing to do with whether or not the mother ate right, did drugs, abused alcohol, smoked cigarettes, was involved in an accident of some sort, or had generalized anxiety while pregnant. More often than not, I have found that mothers tend to be more accepting of their sons' desires to transition to female and fathers tend to be more accepting of their daughters' wanting to transition to male.

One issue which may arise during the coming out phase of transition is how to deal with spouses and children. Of course, the spouse should be told first, though that does not always work out in a positive way. It takes a special relationship of unconditional love to survive the intensity of learning about a spouse's transsexuality. Yet, many couples do find a way for the marriage to survive even this immense change. When it comes to telling children, frankly the younger the children the more likely they are to accept their parent's transition. If the non-trans spouse can model unconditional love for the transitioning spouse, this will normalize the transition in the eyes of the children, who will likely follow suit. Young children, and by that I mean under age ten or so, have not yet learned all the rules of society and tend to accept a parent who changes gender identity.

Some spouses who do not understand feel rejected and angry themselves, and sometimes try to turn the children against the transsexual parent -- especially if the children are in their early to late teens. The children may begin to feel their transsexual parent does not want to be their parent. The older children also wonder how they are going to tell their friends and, even more important, how they will be given away in marriage if it is their father who is transitioning. For the children, this can cause terrible ambivalence. They begin questioning the transsexual parent in a way which causes a great deal of guilt in that parent. It is so difficult to be a parent and take care of oneself when the need to transition feels like a matter of life and death, while, at the same time, the guilt they feel from their children's negative response is also very strong. Some of my clients have put aside their transition to raise their children first in the hope that, as their children become adults, they will have a better ability to understand.

When I meet with parents of a transsexual child, I try to help them understand what it means to be a transsexual -- to feel as though one is born in the wrong body and to need to change that body in order to feel right.  I always work at not betraying the client's confidentiality and just answer parents' general questions about the requirements for transition by explaining the Harry Benjamin Standards of Care.  These were developed in the late 1950s to help professionals and transsexuals work together on the upcoming transition.

Transitioning from one gender to another is probably the most stigmatized avenue to take in one's life.  It is not a decision made lightly.  If telling family, friends and work colleagues about the upcoming transition is not done in a healthy way, one is setting himself or herself up for failure.  The goal of all therapists who work with transsexual clients should be to help each client make his or her transition in a way in which maximum long-term comfort can be achieved for all, understanding that there may be some lost relationships along the way.  With increased awareness and careful planning, loss of relationships can be minimized and the transgender client can go on to a happier life than he or she ever thought possible.

Together we can make the world better, one person at a time.
-- Sheila Mink

# GLOSSARY OF TRANSGENDER TERMS

**Crossdresser:** Someone who feels the need to express his or her other gender, at least part-time. Usually refers to heterosexual males, but there are females who crossdress as well. Former term: transvestite.

**FTM or MTF:** Transgendered persons may be female-to-male or male-to-female or may, occasionally, prefer to live inbetween the two usual genders.

**Gender:** The traditional social concept that everyone is either male or female, is usually based on the infant's genitalia, but also includes many social and sexual role prescriptions.

**Gender Dysphoria:** Feelings of pain, anguish, and anxiety that arise from the mismatch between a trans person's physical sex and his or her internal gender identity.

**Gender Identity:** One's own personal sense of being a man or a woman, a boy or a girl or, occasionally, something inbetween. (Not to be confused with sexual orientation.)

**Gender Queer:** A term used by some of the younger trans people; it avoids being boxed into either the male or female gender.

**Gender Transition:** The period when transsexual (and sometimes transgenderist ) persons change their bodies in order to facilitate living their lives in the social role congruent with their bodies.

**Hormonal Sex Reassignment:** Administration of estrogens (for male to female transsexuals) or androgens (for female to male transsexuals) to promote the development of secondary sexual characteristics of the other sex.

**Intersexed:** The preferred term for persons born with ambiguous genitalia and/or chromosomal anomalies. Many intersexed infants and children have their ambiguous genitalia surgically "normalized" (altered), often resulting in the loss of sexual response and/or assignment to the wrong gender. Former term: Hermaphrodite.

**Real Life Test (RLT):** (also called the Real Life Experi-ence or Living Full-time) The one-year minimum period when transsexual persons must be able to demonstrate to their psychotherapist their ability to live successfully and work full-time in their congruent gender, a prerequisite for sex reassignment surgery (SRS), as mandated by the Standards of Care.

**Sex:** The state of biological maleness or femaleness identified at birth, as opposed to gender identity, which children seem to experience, or self-identify, at a very early age.

**Sex Reassignment:** Hormonal and surgical modification of the body to make it resemble, as much as possible, that of the other sex, in order to facilitate living in the social role matching one's true gender identity.

**Sex Reassignment Surgery (SRS):** Permanent surgical refashioning of the genitalia to resemble the external genitalia of the other sex.

**Sexual Orientation:** Sexual attraction to persons of the same, opposite, or either sex. A person may be heterosexual, homosexual, bisexual, asexual or self-sexual.

**Si, Hir:** New pronouns coined to avoid the male/female dichotomy, Si replaces she/he and hir replaces him/her.

**SOFFA:** A recently coined umbrella term referring to significant others, family members, friends and allies.

**Standards of Care:** A set of guidelines formulated by the Harry Benjamin International Gender Dysphoria Association intended to

172

safeguard both transsexual persons and those who provide professional services.

**Top surgery:**   Breast removal for female-to-male transsexuals, as opposed to "bottom (genital) surgery".

**Transgendered:**  Any person whose gender identity, expression, or behaviors are not traditionally associated with their birth sex. While not accepted by everyone, this term is widely used to designate the full spectrum of people with gender issues. (Other forms include transgenders or trans persons.)

**Transgenderists:**   A term often used to refer to those transgendered persons, usually MTF, who choose to live full-time as the other gender without benefit of surgery or, sometimes, even hormones. Other terms: Non-op or non-operative transsexual.

**Transsexuals:** People who are profoundly unhappy in their birth sex and who seek to change, or have already changed, their bodies to match their gender identity. They may be FTM or MTF.

No pessimist ever discovered the secrets of the stars or sailed to an uncharted land or opened a new heaven to the human spirit.          -- Helen Keller (Raqual Rice)

\* \* \*

Paradise is where I am.          -- Voltaire  (Judy Hoff)

# NATIONAL TRANSGENDER
# ORGANIZATIONS AND RESOURCES

PFLAG's T-NET (Transgender Network) provides information and support for both trans persons and their families. For support and resources for adults and families of trans children: (216) 691-HELP (4357), or email: IMATMom@aol.com. To subscribe to the tgs-pflag list, send the following one-line command to tgs-pflag@youth-guard.org (in the body of the message, not the subject line): subscribe tgs-pflag your email address or contact the list owner at maggie@critpath.org. Or contact: maryboenke@aol.com or 180 Bailey Blvd., Hardy, VA 24101

The American Boyz has many local affiliates throughout the US, and provides support and information for female-to-male transgendered persons and their significant others, friends, family members and allies (SOFFAs). The American Boyz, 212A South Bridge Street, Suite 131, Elkton, MD, 21921. Phone: (410)620-2161. Website: www. amboyz.org. Email: amboyz@iximd.com.

FTM International (FTMI) provides support and information for female-to male transsexuals world-wide. FTM International, 1360 Mission Street, Suite 200, San Francisco, CA 94103. Phone: (415) 553-5987. Website: www.ftm-intl.org. Email: TSTGMen@aol.com.

Gender Education and Advocacy (GEA) is the successor organization to AEGIS (American Educational Gender Information Service) with twin missions of gender education and health care advocacy. GEA operates the Gender Advocacy Internet News Service (GAIN). To subscribe to GAIN, go to www.tgender.net/mailman/listinfo/gain-all. GEA National Office, P.O. Box 65, Kensington, MD 20895. Website: www.gender.org.

Harry Benjamin International Gender Dysphoria Association, Inc. (HBIGDA) publishes their Standards of Care for Gender Identity Disorders and conducts a symposium for professional providers and transgendered consumers every other year. HBIGDA, 1300 South 2nd Street, Suite 180, Minneapolis, MN 55454. Phone: (612) 625-9547. Website: www.hbigda.org. Email: hbigda@famprac.umn.edu.

The International Foundation for Gender Education (IFGE) provides telephone information, referrals and books, and publishes the quarterly magazine Transgender Tapestry. IFGE, PO Box 229, Waltham, MA 02254-0229. Phone: (781) 899-2212. Website: www.ifge.org. Email: info@ifge.org.

The Intersex Society of North America (ISNA) provides information, support and advocacy for intersexed people. ISNA, P.O. Box 3070, Ann Arbor, MI 48106-3070. Phone: (734) 994-7369. Website: www.isna.org. Email: info@isna.org.

The National Latino/Latina Lesbian, Gay, Bisexual and Transgender Organization (LLEGO) is an informational resource for Spanish-speakers. LLEGO, 1420 K Street NW, Suite 200, Washington, DC 20006. (202) 408-5380. www.llego.org. Email: aquilgbt@llego.org.

The National Youth Advocacy Coalition (NYAC) focuses on advocacy, education and information for gay, lesbian, bisexual, transgender and questioning youth. NYAC, 1638 R Street, NW, Suite 300, Washington, DC 20009. Phone: (202) 319-7596. Website: www.nyacyouth.org.

The Renaissance Transgender Association, with chapters and affiliates throughout the US, provides support, education and social activities for crossdressers and others. Renaissance Transgender Association, 987 Old Eagle School Rd., Suite 719, Wayne, PA 19087. Phone: (610) 975-9119. Website: www.ren.org. Email: info@ren.org.

The Society for the Second Self (Tri-Ess), with about 30 chapters in the US, focuses on the needs of heterosexual crossdressers. Tri-Ess, P.O. Box 194, Tulare, CA 93275. Email: trisinfo@aol.com.

# TRANSGENDER FAMILY READING LIST

Allen, Mariette Pathy. *Transformations: Crossdressers and Those Who Love Them.* New York: Dutton, 1989.

Bornstein, Kate. *Gender Outlaw: On Men, Women and the Rest of Us.* New York: Routledge, 1994.

Brown, Mildred and Choe Ann Rounsley.*True Selves: Understanding Transsexualism for Family, Friends, Coworkers & Helping Professionals.* San Francisco: Jossey-Bass, 1996.

Bullough, Vernon and Bonnie Bullough. *Crossdressing, Sex and Gender.* Philadelphia: University of Pennsylvania Press, 1993.

Burke, Phyllis. *Gender Shock: Exploding the Myths of Male and Female.* New York: Doubleday, 1996.

Cameron, Loren. *Body Alchemy: Transsexual Portraits.* San Francisco: Cleis Press, 1996.

Colapinto, John. *As Nature Made Him: The Boy Who Was Raised as a Girl.* New York: Harper Collins, 2000.

Currah, P., S. Minter, & J. Green. *Transgender Equality: A Handbook for Activists and Policymakers.* Washington, DC: National Gay and Lesbian Task Force, 2000.

Dreger, Alice. *Intersexed In the Age of Ethics.* Hagerstown, MD: University Publishing Group, 1999.

Ettner, Randi. *Confessions of a Gender Defender: A Psychologist's Reflections on Life Among the Transgendered.* Evanston, IL: Chicago Spectrum, 1996.

Feinberg, Leslie. *Transgendered Warriors: Making History from Joan of Arc to RuPaul.* Boston: Beacon Press, 1996.

Gillespie, P. (Ed.) *Love Makes a Family: Portraits of Gay, Lesbian, Bisexual, and Transgender Parents and Their Families.* Amherst: University of Masschusetts Press, 1999.

Israel, Gianna and Donald Tarver. *Transgender Care: Recommended Guidelines, Practical Information, and Personal Accounts.* Philadelphia: Temple University Press, 1997.

Jorgensen, C. *Christine Jorgensen: A Personal Autobiography.* San Francisco: Cleis Press, 2001.

Just Evelyn. *Mom, I Need To Be A Girl.* Imperial Beach, CA: Walter Trook Publishing, 1998. Or see www.justevelyn.com

Kirk, Sheila and Martine Rothblatt. *Medical, Legal and Workplace Issues for the Transsexual.* Watertown, MA: Together Lifeworks, 1995.

Meyerowitz, Joanne. *How Sex Changed: A History Of Transsexuality In The United States.* Cambridge: Harvard University Press, 2002.

Minter, Shannon. *Issues for Transgendered Parents.* San Francisco: National Center for Lesbian Rights, 2000. (Available for $20 from NCLR, 870 Market Street, Suite 570, San Francisco, CA 94102).

Morris, J. *Conundrum: An Extraordinary Narrative of Transsexualism.* New York: Harcourt Brace Jovanovich, 1974. Reprinted by Coronet in 1975.

Pratt, Minnie Bruce. *S/He.* Ithaca, NY: Firebrand Books, 1995.

Preiss, Irene. *Fixed for Life: The True Saga of How Tom Became Sally.* Lincoln, NE: iUniverse.com, 1999.

Rudd, Peggy. Crossdressers and Those Who Share Their Lives.

Katy, TX: PM Publishers, 1995.

Scholinski, Daphne. *The Last Time I Wore a Dress.* New York: Riverhead Books, 1997.

Stuart, Kim. *The Uninvited Dilemma: A Question of Gender.* Portland, OR: Revised Edition, Metamorphous Press, 1991.

Sullivan, Lou. *Information* for *the Female-To-Male Crossdresser and Transsexual.* Seattle: Ingersoll Gender Center, 1990.

Walworth, Janis. *Transsexual Workers: An Empoyer's Guide.* Los Angeles: The Center for Gender Sanity, 1998.

Walworth, Janis. *Working With a Transsexual: A Guide for Coworkers.* Los Angeles: The Center for Gender Sanity, 1998.

Whittle, Stephen. *The White Book: The Trans Man's Survival Guide.* London: FTM Network, 1998

Wilchins, Riki. *Read My Lips.* Ithaca, NY: Firebrand Books, 1997

*** 

## HOW TO ORDER THIS BOOK

You may order copies of this book from Oak Knoll Press, 180 Bailey Blvd., Hardy, VA 24101. $13.95, including shipping in the USA. Amazon.com and many gay book stores will probably carry the book again. For shipping out of country, quantity or wholesale prices, please email maryboenke@aol.com or see www.aiyiyi.com/transbook.

## CONNECTING WITH AUTHORS

I am happy to receive readers' comments or to forward any surface or email to any authors/poets in this book or on the back cover. Many are eager to hear from readers or to receive requests for services. Use contact information just above. -- MMB